Hydrologic Conditions in New Hampshire and Vermont, Water Year 2011

By Richard G. Kiah, Jason D. Jarvis, Robert F. Hegemann, Gregory S. Hilgendorf, and Sanborn L. Ward

Prepared in cooperation with the
States of New Hampshire and Vermont and with other agencies

Open-File Report 2013–1135

U.S. Department of the Interior
U.S. Geological Survey

U.S. Department of the Interior
SALLY JEWELL, Secretary

U.S. Geological Survey
Suzette M. Kimball, Acting Director

U.S. Geological Survey, Reston, Virginia: 2013

For more information on the USGS—the Federal source for science about the Earth, its natural and living resources, natural hazards, and the environment, visit http://www.usgs.gov or call 1–888–ASK–USGS.

For an overview of USGS information products, including maps, imagery, and publications, visit http://www.usgs.gov/pubprod

To order this and other USGS information products, visit http://store.usgs.gov

Suggested citation:
Kiah, R.G., Jarvis, J.D., Hegemann, R.F., Hilgendorf, G.S., and Ward, S.L., 2013, Hydrologic conditions in New Hampshire and Vermont, water year 2011: U.S. Geological Survey Open-File Report 2013–1135, 36 p., http://pubs.usgs.gov/of/2013/1135/.

Contents

Figures

Tables

Conversion Factors and Datum

Inch/Pound to SI

Multiply	By	To obtain
Length		
inch (in.)	2.54	centimeter (cm)
foot (ft)	0.3048	meter (m)
Area		
square mile (mi^2)	2.590	square kilometer (km^2)
Flow rate		
cubic foot per second (ft^3/s)	0.02832	cubic meter per second (m^3/s)

Horizontal coordinate information is referenced to the North American Datum of 1983 (NAD 83).

Vertical coordinate information is referenced to the National Geodetic Vertical Datum of 1929 (NGVD 29).

Elevation, as used in this report, refers to distance above the vertical datum.

Hydrologic Conditions in New Hampshire and Vermont, Water Year 2011

By Richard G. Kiah, Jason D. Jarvis, Robert F. Hegemann, Gregory S. Hilgendorf, and Sanborn L. Ward

Abstract

Record-high hydrologic conditions in New Hampshire and Vermont occurred during water year 2011, according to data from 125 streamgages and lake gaging stations, 27 crest-stage gages, and 41 groundwater wells. Annual runoff for the 2011 water year was the sixth highest on record for New Hampshire and the highest on record for Vermont on the basis of a 111-year reference period (water years 1901–2011). Groundwater levels for the 2011 water year were generally normal in New Hampshire and normal to above normal in Vermont.

Record flooding occurred in April, May, and August of water year 2011. Peak-of-record streamflows were recorded at 38 streamgages, 25 of which had more than 10 years of record. Flooding in April 2011 was widespread in parts of northern New Hampshire and Vermont; peak-of-record streamflows were recorded at nine streamgages. Flash flooding in May 2011 was isolated to central and northeastern Vermont; peak-of-record streamflows were recorded at five streamgages. Devastating flooding in August 2011 occurred throughout most of Vermont and in parts of New Hampshire as a result of the heavy rains associated with Tropical Storm Irene. Peak-of-record streamflows were recorded at 24 streamgages.

Introduction

The U.S. Geological Survey, in cooperation with State agencies, obtains a large amount of data pertaining to the water resources of New Hampshire and Vermont each water year[1]. These data, accumulated during many water years, constitute a valuable database for developing an improved understanding of the water resources of the two States. To make these data readily available to interested parties outside the U.S. Geological Survey, they are published annually and are available online at http://water.usgs.gov.

---

[1]A water year is the 12-month period October 1 through September 30. It is designated by the calendar year in which it ends and which includes 9 of the 12 months.

Record-high hydrologic conditions in New Hampshire and Vermont occurred during water year 2011. Major flooding was documented in April, May, and August. Widespread damage caused by the flooding led President Barack H. Obama to declare major disasters in parts of New Hampshire for the floods in May and August and in parts of Vermont for floods in April, May, and August.

Purpose and Scope

This report summarizes hydrologic conditions and flooding in New Hampshire and Vermont for water year 2011. Records of stage and flow of streams, contents of lakes and reservoirs, and water levels of groundwater wells are included. In water year 2011, hydrologic data were collected at 125 streamgages and lake gaging stations, 27 crest-stage gages, and 41 groundwater wells. The severity of record floods in water year 2011 is summarized in terms of annual peak streamflows related to historical peak streamflows at selected streamgages.

Historical Records

Prior to 1960, water-resources data for New Hampshire and Vermont were published in U.S. Geological Survey Water-Supply Papers. Data on streamflow and stage and on lake or reservoir contents and stage, through September 1960, were published annually under the title "Surface-Water Supply of the United States, Parts 1A and 1B." For the 1961 through 1970 water years, the data were published in two 5-year reports. Data on chemical quality, temperature, and suspended sediment for the 1941 through 1970 water years were published annually under the title "Quality of Surface Waters of the United States," and data on water levels for the 1939 through 1974 water years were published under the title "Ground-Water Levels in the United States."

From 1961 to 1974, surface-water quantity data for New Hampshire and Vermont were published in annual reports as "Water Resources Data for Massachusetts, New Hampshire, Rhode Island, and Vermont." For the 1964 water year, a similar report was introduced that contained only data relating to water quality. Beginning with the 1975 water year, the report format was changed to present, in one volume, data on quantities of surface water, quality of surface water and groundwater, and groundwater levels. These official reports have an identification number consisting of the two-letter State abbreviation, the last two digits of the water year, and the volume number. For example, the water year 2005 volume is identified as "U.S. Geological Survey Water-Data Report NH–VT–05–1."

Publication of site-specific data pages began in water year 2006. Data pages for individual sites published by the U.S. Geological Survey for all States are available on the Internet at http://wdr.water.usgs.gov/.

Real-time and historical data from the surface-water network, as well as information about individual sites, are available through the Internet at http://waterdata.usgs.gov/usa/nwis/rt.

Cooperators for Data Collection in New Hampshire and Vermont

The U.S. Geological Survey and organizations of the States of New Hampshire and Vermont have had cooperative agreements for the systematic collection of surface-water data since the early 1900s, and for groundwater data since the mid-1960s. Organizations that assisted in collecting the data in this report through cooperative agreements with the U.S. Geological Survey are

- New Hampshire Department of Environmental Services;

- Vermont Department of Environmental Conservation;

- Vermont Department of Forests, Parks, and Recreation;

- Vermont Agency of Transportation;

- Maine Emergency Management;

- Maine River Flow Advisory Commission;

- New England Interstate Water Pollution Control Commission;

- City of Keene, N.H.;

- City of Rochester, N.H.;

- Town of Salem, N.H.;

- Lake Champlain Basin Program;

- City of South Burlington, Vt.;

- City of Montpelier, Vt.; and

- Town of Burke, Vt.

Assistance in the form of funds or services was provided by the U.S. Army Corps of Engineers for the collection of data at 19 streamgages in 2011. Organizations supplying data are

acknowledged in the National Water Information System: Web Interface.

The following organizations contributed funds and services through the requirements of the Federal Energy Regulatory Commission:

- Green Mountain Power Company,

- Great Bay Hydro Corporation,

- Public Service Company of New Hampshire, and

- Florida Power and Light Company.

Hydrologic Conditions in New Hampshire and Vermont, Water Year 2011

Hydrologic conditions in New Hampshire and Vermont were characterized through the use of data from 125 streamgages and lake gaging stations, 27 crest-stage gages, and 41 groundwater wells (figs. 1 and 2, tables 1 and 2). This section describes hydrologic conditions in terms of precipitation, streamflow, lake and reservoir elevations, and groundwater levels.

Precipitation

During the 2011 water year, precipitation trends for the States of New Hampshire and Vermont were observed at the upper end of historical levels. An abnormally high snowpack during the 2010–11 winter, spring thunderstorms, and Tropical Storm Irene in August resulted in the third highest annual accumulated precipitation in New Hampshire and the highest level ever recorded in Vermont, according to precipitation data collected by the National Oceanic and Atmospheric Administration since 1895 (National Oceanic and Atmospheric Administration, 2011).

New Hampshire has experienced an increase in precipitation trends over the past 5 years with the top 3 years of annual accumulated precipitation on record occurring during water years 2006–2011 (National Oceanic and Atmospheric Administration, 2011). Water year 2006 had the highest annual accumulated precipitation of 66.65 inches (in.), followed by 2008 at 59.94 in. and 2011 at 57.70 in. Accumulated annual precipitation for the 2011 water year in Vermont was 62.46 in.; the second highest accumulated precipitation was 58.44 in. in water year 1928.

Snowpack data collected by New Hampshire Department of Environmental Services (2011) and the U.S. Army Corps of Engineers (2011) show region-wide snow-water equivalents reaching 7 in. at the height of the 2010–11 winter snowpack. The snowpack had an average water equivalent of 5 in. by April 1, 2011, and was completely gone by the end of the month (National Weather Service, 2011).

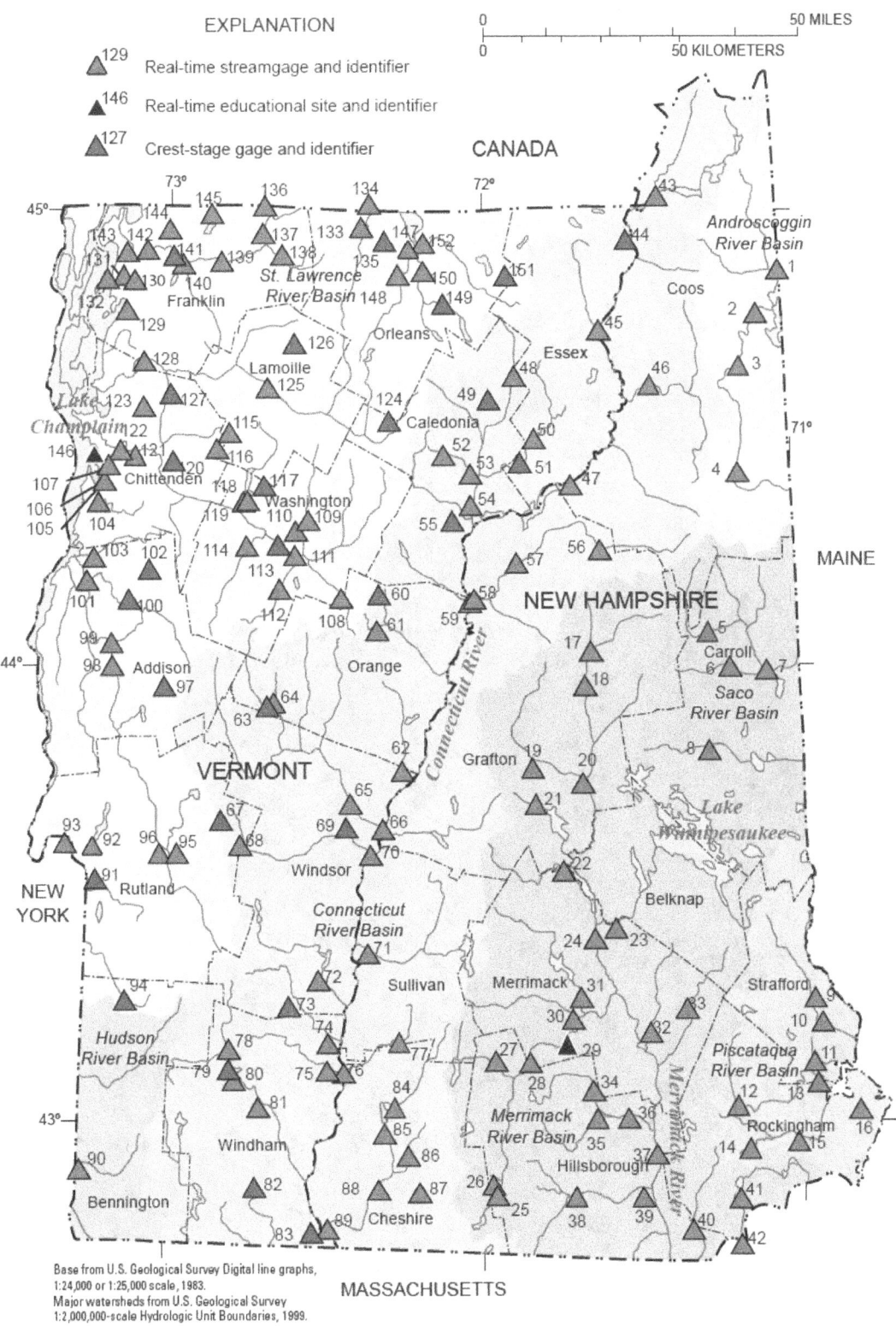

Figure 1.   U.S. Geological Survey surface-water gaging stations in New Hampshire and Vermont.

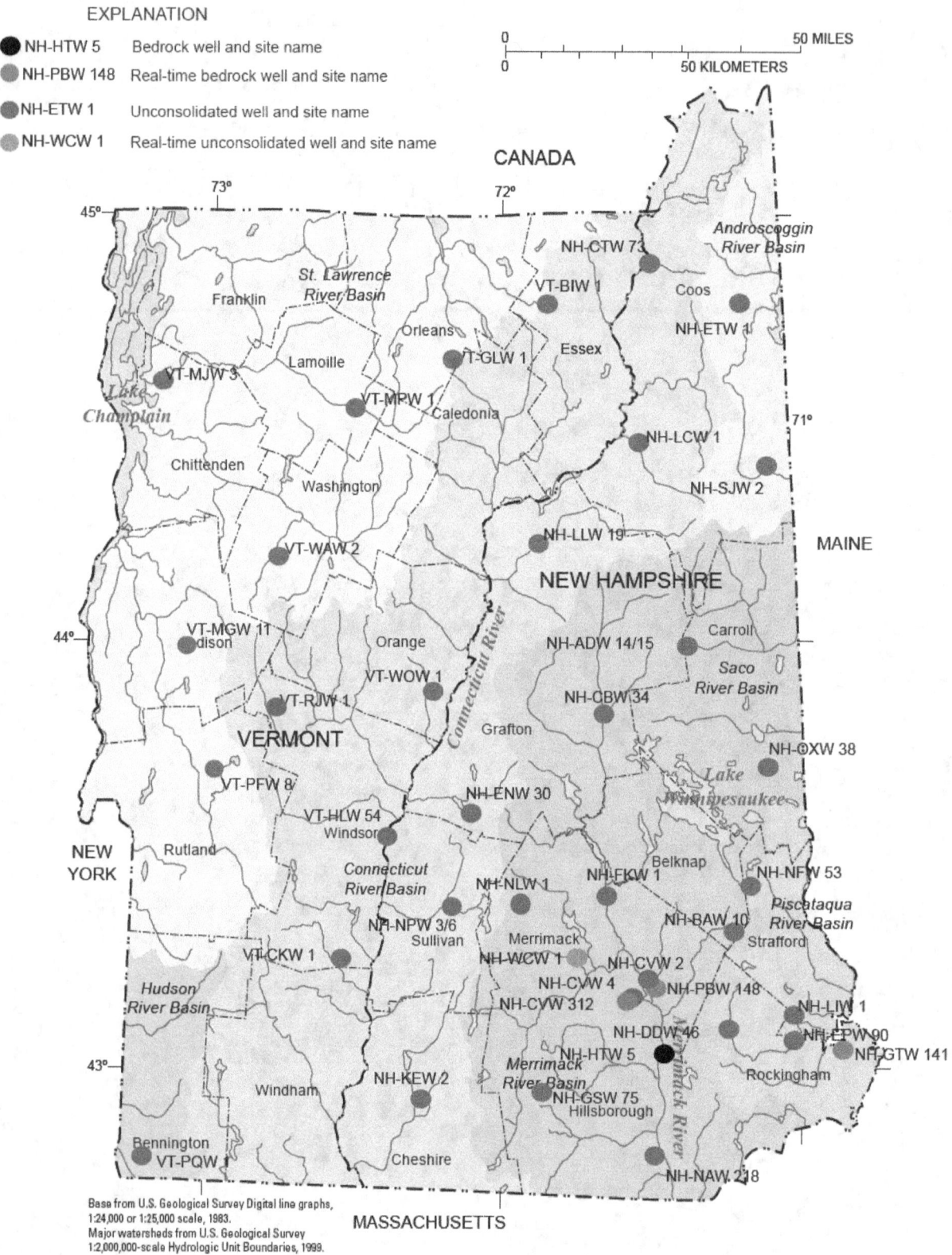

EXPLANATION

● NH-HTW 5   Bedrock well and site name

● NH-PBW 148   Real-time bedrock well and site name

● NH-ETW 1   Unconsolidated well and site name

● NH-WCW 1   Real-time unconsolidated well and site name

Base from U.S. Geological Survey Digital line graphs,
1:24,000 or 1:25,000 scale, 1983.
Major watersheds from U.S. Geological Survey
1:2,000,000-scale Hydrologic Unit Boundaries, 1999.

Figure 2.   U.S. Geological Survey groundwater wells in New Hampshire and Vermont.

Table 1. Description of streamgages in New Hampshire and Vermont

[mi², square mile; na, not applicable; NH, New Hampshire; MA, Massachusetts; VT, Vermont; misc , miscellaneous]

Site	Station number	Station name	Drainage area mi²)	Record type
		Androscoggin River Basin		
1	01052500	DIAMOND RIVER NEAR WENTWORTH LOCATION, NH	152	Discharge
2	01053500	ANDROSCOGGIN RIVER AT ERROL, NH	1,046	Discharge
3	01053600	ANDROSCOGGIN RIVER BELOW BOG BROOK AT CAMBRIDGE, NH	1,177	Discharge
4	01054000	ANDROSCOGGIN RIVER NEAR GORHAM, NH	1,361	Discharge
		Saco River Basin		
5	010642505	SACO RIVER AT RIVER STREET, AT BARTLETT, NH	91	Discharge
6	01064485	SWIFT RIVER 0.5 MI BELOW HOBBS BR, NR CONWAY, NH	76.8	Discharge
7	01064500	SACO RIVER NEAR CONWAY, NH	385	Discharge
8	01064801	BEARCAMP RIVER AT SOUTH TAMWORTH, NH	67.6	Discharge
		Piscataquo River Basin		
9	01072800	COCHECO RIVER NEAR ROCHESTER, NH	85.7	Discharge
10	01072870	ISINGLASS R AT ROCHESTER NECK RD, NR DOVER, NH	73.6	Discharge
11	01073000	OYSTER RIVER NEAR DURHAM, NH	12.1	Discharge
12	01073319	LAMPREY RIVER AT LANGFORD ROAD, AT RAYMOND, NH	55.7	Discharge
13	01073500	LAMPREY RIVER NEAR NEWMARKET, NH	183	Discharge
14	010735562	EXETER RIVER AT ODELL ROAD, NEAR SANDOWN, NH	16.1	Discharge
15	01073587	EXETER RIVER AT HAIGH ROAD, NEAR BRENTWOOD, NH	63.5	Discharge
16	01073785	WINNICUT RIVER AT GREENLAND, NR PORTSMOUTH, NH	14.1	Discharge
		Merrimack River Basin		
17	01074520	EAST BRANCH PEMIGEWASSET RIVER AT LINCOLN, NH	115	Discharge
18	01075000	PEMIGEWASSET RIVER AT WOODSTOCK, NH	193	Discharge
19	01076000	BAKER RIVER NEAR RUMNEY, NH	143	Discharge
20	01076500	PEMIGEWASSET RIVER AT PLYMOUTH, NH	622	Discharge
21	01077400	COCKERMOUTH RIVER BELOW HARDY BROOK, AT GROTON, NH	21.4	Discharge
22	01078000	SMITH RIVER NEAR BRISTOL, NH	85.8	Discharge
23	01081000	WINNIPESAUKEE RIVER AT TILTON, NH	471	Discharge
24	01081500	MERRIMACK RIVER AT FRANKLIN JUNCTION, NH	1,507	Discharge
25	01082000	CONTOOCOOK RIVER AT PETERBOROUGH, NH	68.1	Discharge
26	01083000	NUBANUSIT BK BLW MACDOWELL DAM NR PETERBOROUGH NH	44	Peak discharge
27	01084000	NORTH BRANCH RIVER NEAR ANTRIM, NH	54.8	Discharge
28	01085000	CONTOOCOOK RIVER NEAR HENNIKER, NH	368	Peak discharge
29	01085500	CONTOOCOOK R BL HOPKINTON DAM AT W HOPKINTON, NH	427	Discharge
30	01086000	WARNER RIVER AT DAVISVILLE, NH	146	Discharge
31	01087000	BLACKWATER RIVER NEAR WEBSTER, NH	129	Peak discharge
32	01089100	SOUCOOK RIVER, AT PEMBROKE ROAD, NEAR CONCORD, NH	81.9	Discharge
33	01089500	SUNCOOK RIVER AT NORTH CHICHESTER, NH	157	Discharge
34	01090800	PISCATAQUOG RIVER BL EVERETT DAM, NR E WEARE, NH	63.1	Peak discharge
35	01091000	SOUTH BRANCH PISCATAQUOG RIVER NEAR GOFFSTOWN, NH	104	Discharge
36	01091500	PISCATAQUOG RIVER NEAR GOFFSTOWN, NH	202	Peak discharge
37	01092000	MERRIMACK R NR GOFFS FALLS, BELOW MANCHESTER, NH	3,092	Discharge

Table 1. Description of streamgages in New Hampshire and Vermont.—Continued

[mi², square mile; na, not applicable; NH, New Hampshire; MA, Massachusetts; VT, Vermont; misc., miscellaneous]

Site	Station number	Station name	Drainage area (mi²)	Record type
		Merrimack River Basin—Continued		
38	01093852	SOUHEGAN RIVER (SITE WLR-1) NEAR MILFORD, NH	103	Discharge
39	01094000	SOUHEGAN RIVER AT MERRIMACK, NH	171	Discharge
40	010965852	BEAVER BROOK AT NORTH PELHAM, NH	47.8	Discharge
41	01100505	SPICKET RIVER AT NORTH SALEM, NH	16.5	Discharge
42	01100561	SPICKET RIVER NEAR METHUEN, MA	62.1	Discharge
		Connecticut River Basin		
43	01129200	CONNECTICUT R BELOW INDIAN STREAM NR PITTSBURG, NH	254	Discharge
44	01129420	CAPON BROOK AT VT 102, NEAR CANAAN, VT	4.71	Peak discharge
45	01129500	CONNECTICUT RIVER AT NORTH STRATFORD, NH	799	Discharge
46	01130000	UPPER AMMONOOSUC RIVER NEAR GROVETON, NH	232	Discharge
47	01131500	CONNECTICUT RIVER NEAR DALTON, NH	1,514	Discharge
48	01133000	EAST BRANCH PASSUMPSIC RIVER NEAR EAST HAVEN, VT	53.8	Discharge
49	01133200	QUIMBY BROOK NEAR LYNDONVILLE, VT	2.32	Peak discharge
50	01134500	MOOSE RIVER AT VICTORY, VT	75.2	Discharge
51	01134800	KIRBY BROOK AT CONCORD, VT	8.05	Peak discharge
52	01135150	POPE BROOK (SITE W-3) NEAR NORTH DANVILLE, VT	3.25	Discharge
53	01135300	SLEEPERS RIVER (SITE W-5) NEAR ST. JOHNSBURY, VT	42.9	Discharge
54	01135500	PASSUMPSIC RIVER AT PASSUMPSIC, VT	436	Discharge
55	01135700	JOES BROOK TRIBUTARY NEAR EAST BARNET, VT	0.76	Peak discharge
56	01137500	AMMONOOSUC RIVER AT BETHLEHEM JUNCTION, NH	87.6	Discharge
57	01137940	AMMONOOSUC RIVER BELOW LISBON DAM, AT LISBON, NH	288	Discharge
58	01138500	CONNECTICUT RIVER AT WELLS RIVER, VT	2,644	Discharge
59	01139000	WELLS RIVER AT WELLS RIVER, VT	98.4	Discharge
60	01139700	WAITS RIVER TRIBUTARY NEAR WEST TOPSHAM, VT	1.09	Peak discharge
61	01139800	EAST ORANGE BRANCH AT EAST ORANGE, VT	8.95	Discharge
62	01141500	OMPOMPANOOSUC RIVER AT UNION VILLAGE, VT	130	Peak discharge
63	01142400	THIRD BRANCH WHITE RIVER TRIBUTARY AT RANDOLPH, VT	0.77	Peak discharge
64	01142500	AYERS BROOK AT RANDOLPH, VT	30.5	Discharge
65	01144000	WHITE RIVER AT WEST HARTFORD, VT	690	Discharge
66	01144500	CONNECTICUT RIVER AT WEST LEBANON, NH	4,092	Discharge
67	01150800	KENT BROOK NEAR KILLINGTON, VT	3.31	Peak discharge
68	01150900	OTTAUQUECHEE RIVER NEAR WEST BRIDGEWATER, VT	23.4	Peak discharge
69	01151200	OTTAUQUECHEE RIVET TRIBUTARY NEAR QUECHEE, VT	0.82	Peak discharge
70	01151500	OTTAUQUECHEE RIVER AT NORTH HARTLAND, VT	221	Discharge
71	01152500	SUGAR RIVER AT WEST CLAREMONT, NH	269	Discharge
72	01153000	BLACK RIVER AT NORTH SPRINGFIELD, VT	158	Peak discharge
73	01153300	MIDDLE BRANCH WILLIAMS RIVER TRIBUTARY AT CHESTER, VT	3.16	Peak discharge
74	01153550	WILLIAMS RIVER NEAR ROCKINGHAM VT	112	Discharge
75	01154000	SAXTONS RIVER AT SAXTONS RIVER, VT	72.2	Discharge
76	01154500	CONNECTICUT RIVER AT NORTH WALPOLE, NH	5,493	Discharge

Table 1. Description of streamgages in New Hampshire and Vermont.—Continued

[mi², square mile; na, not applicable; NH, New Hampshire; MA, Massachusetts; VT, Vermont; misc , miscellaneous]

Site	Station number	Station name	Drainage area (mi²)	Record type
		Connecticut River Basin—Continued		
77	01154950	COLD RIVER AT HIGH STREET, AT ALSTEAD, NH	74.6	Discharge
78	01155349	WEST RIVER BELOW WINHALL RIVER, NEAR JAMAICA, VT	161	Misc. measurements
79	01155350	WEST RIVER TRIBUTARY AT RT 30, NEAR JAMAICA, VT	0.9	Peak discharge
80	01155500	WEST RIVER AT JAMAICA, VT	179	Discharge
81	01155910	WEST RIVER BELOW TOWNSHEND DAM NEAR TOWNSHEND, VT	282	Peak discharge
82	01156300	WHETSTONE BROOK TRIBUTARY NEAR MARLBORO, VT	1.05	Peak discharge
83	01156450	CONNECTICUT RIVER TRIBUTARY NEAR VERNON, VT	1.12	Peak discharge
84	01157000	ASHUELOT RIVER NEAR GILSUM, NH	71.1	Discharge
85	01158000	ASHUELOT RIVER BELOW SURRY MT DAM, NEAR KEENE, NH	101	Discharge
86	01158600	OTTER BROOK BELOW OTTER BROOK DAM, NEAR KEENE, NH	47.2	Peak discharge
87	01160000	S BR ASHUELOT RIVER AT WEBB, NR MARLBOROUGH, NH	36	Discharge
88	01160350	ASHUELOT RIVER AT WEST SWANZEY, NH	316	Discharge
89	01161000	ASHUELOT RIVER AT HINSDALE, NH	420	Discharge
		Hudson River Basin		
90	01334000	WALLOOMSAC RIVER NEAR NORTH BENNINGTON, VT	111	Discharge
		St. Lawrence River Basin		
91	04279400	POULTNEY RIVER TRIBUTARY AT EAST POULTNEY, VT	1.13	Peak discharge
92	04279490	LAKE BOMOSEEN AT OUTLET, NEAR FAIR HAVEN, VT	37.5	Stage
93	04280000	POULTNEY RIVER BELOW FAIR HAVEN, VT	187	Discharge
94	04280240	METTAWEE RIVER TRIBUTARY NO. 3 AT VT 30, AT EAST RUPERT, VT	2.59	Peak discharge
95	04280910	MOON BROOK BELOW MUSSEY BROOK AT RUTLAND, VT	8.29	Discharge
96	04282000	OTTER CREEK AT CENTER RUTLAND, VT	307	Discharge
97	04282300	BRANDY BROOK AT BREAD LOAF, VT	2.24	Peak discharge
98	04282500	OTTER CREEK AT MIDDLEBURY, VT	628	Discharge
99	04282525	NEW HAVEN RIVER AT BROOKSVILLE, NR MIDDLEBURY, VT	115	Discharge
100	04282600	LITTLE OTTER CREEK TRIBUTARY NEAR BRISTOL, VT	1.48	Peak discharge
101	04282650	LITTLE OTTER CREEK AT FERRISBURG, VT.	57.1	Discharge
102	04282700	LEWIS CREEK TRIBUTARY AT STARKSBORO, VT	5.31	Peak discharge
103	04282780	LEWIS CREEK AT NORTH FERRISBURG, VT.	77.2	Discharge
104	04282795	LAPLATTE RIVER AT SHELBURNE FALLS, VT.	44.6	Discharge
105	04282800	MUNROE BROOK AT SHELBURNE, VT	5.35	Discharge
106	04282805	BARTLETT BROOK AT SOUTH BURLINGTON, VT	1.04	Discharge
107	04282813	POTASH BR AT QUEEN CITY PARK RD, NR BURLINGTON, VT	7.18	Discharge
108	04283500	EAST BARRE DETENTION RESERVOIR AT EAST BARRE, VT	38.8	Stage
109	04285000	WRIGHTSVILLE DETENTION RESERVOIR AT WRIGHTSVILLE, VT	66.5	Stage
110	04285500	NORTH BRANCH WINOOSKI RIVER AT WRIGHTSVILLE, VT	69.2	Discharge
111	04286000	WINOOSKI RIVER AT MONTPELIER, VT	397	Discharge
112	04287000	DOG RIVER AT NORTHFIELD FALLS, VT	76.1	Discharge
113	04287300	SUNNY BROOK NEAR MONTPELIER, VT	2.31	Peak discharge
114	04288000	MAD RIVER NEAR MORETOWN, VT	139	Discharge

Table 1.   Description of streamgages in New Hampshire and Vermont.—Continued

[mi², square mile; na, not applicable; NH, New Hampshire; MA, Massachusetts; VT, Vermont; misc., miscellaneous]

Site	Station number	Station name	Drainage area (mi²)	Record type
		St. Lawrence River Basin—Continued		
115	04288225	W BRANCH LITTLE R ABV BINGHAM FALLS NEAR STOWE, VT	4.67	Discharge
116	04288230	RANCH BROOK AT RANCH CAMP, NEAR STOWE, VT	3.8	Discharge
117	04288400	BRYANT BROOK AT WATERBURY CENTER, VT	2.64	Peak discharge
118	04288500	WATERBURY RESERVOIR NEAR WATERBURY, VT	109	Stage
119	04289000	LITTLE RIVER NEAR WATERBURY, VT	111	Discharge
120	04289600	WINOOSKI RIVER TRIBUTARY NEAR RICHMOND, VT	0.71	Peak discharge
121	04290335	ALLEN BROOK AT VT 2A, NEAR ESSEX JUNCTION, VT	9.9	Discharge
122	04290500	WINOOSKI RIVER NEAR ESSEX JUNCTION, VT	1,044	Discharge
123	04290575	INDIAN BROOK NEAR ESSEX JUNCTION, VT	6.48	Discharge
124	04290700	BAILEY BROOK AT EAST HARDWICK, VT	2.52	Peak discharge
125	04292000	LAMOILLE RIVER AT JOHNSON, VT	310	Discharge
126	04292100	STONY BROOK NEAR EDEN, VT	4.21	Peak discharge
127	04292355	MORGAN BR TRIB AT OLD NO 11 RD, NEAR WESTFORD, VT	2.15	Peak discharge
128	04292500	LAMOILLE RIVER AT EAST GEORGIA, VT	686	Discharge
129	04292750	MILL RIVER AT GEORGIA SHORE RD, NR ST ALBANS, VT	22.3	Discharge
130	04292770	STEVENS BROOK AT LEMNAH DRIVE, AT ST ALBANS, VT	1.54	Discharge
131	04292795	STEVENS BROOK AT KELLOGG ROAD, NEAR ST. ALBANS, VT	6.95	Discharge
132	04292810	JEWETT BROOK AT VT 38, NEAR ST. ALBANS, VT	3.74	Discharge
133	04293000	MISSISQUOI RIVER NEAR NORTH TROY, VT	131	Discharge
134	04293200	MUD CREEK AT BEAR MOUNTAIN RD, NEAR NORTH TROY, VT	37.1	Discharge
135	04293005	DUNN BROOK AT VT100, NEAR NEWPORT CENTER, VT	2.85	Peak discharge
136	04293430	NORTH BRANCH ABOVE RIVER STREET, AT RICHFORD, VT	64.8	Discharge
137	04293500	MISSISQUOI RIVER NEAR EAST BERKSHIRE, VT	479	Discharge
138	04293600	TROUT RIVER AT HOPKINS BR, NR ENOSBURG FALLS, VT	78.6	Discharge
139	04293700	TYLER BRANCH AT DUFFY HILL RD NR ENOSBURG FALLS, VT	55.1	Discharge
140	04293795	BLACK CREEK ABOVE BRIDGE STREET, AT SHELDON, VT	119	Discharge
141	04293800	MISSISIQUOI RIVER TRIBUTARY AT SHELDON JUNCTION, VT	1.69	Peak discharge
142	04293900	HUNGERFORD BR AT HIGHGATE RD NR HIGHGATE CENTER, VT	18.6	Discharge
143	04294000	MISSISQUOI RIVER AT SWANTON, VT	850	Discharge
144	04294140	ROCK RIVER NEAR HIGHGATE CENTER, VT	11.3	Discharge
145	04294300	PIKE RIVER AT EAST FRANKLIN, NR ENOSBURG FALLS, VT	34.5	Discharge
146	04294500	LAKE CHAMPLAIN AT BURLINGTON, VT	na	Stage
147	04295500	LAKE MEMPHREMAGOG AT NEWPORT, VT	na	Stage
148	04296000	BLACK RIVER AT COVENTRY, VT	122	Discharge
149	04296150	LORD BROOK NEAR EVANSVILLE, VT	4.76	Peak discharge
150	04296280	BARTON RIVER NEAR COVENTRY, VT	155	Discharge
151	04296300	PHERRINS RIVER TRIBUTARY NEAR ISLAND POND, VT	1.05	Peak discharge
152	04296500	CLYDE RIVER AT NEWPORT, VT	142	Discharge

Table 2. Description of groundwater wells in New Hampshire and Vermont.

[Site name, U.S. Geological Survey local well number based on State, town, and a sequential number; Well depth, in feet below land surface datum; ft, feet]

Site number	Site name	County	Well depth (ft)	Local aquifer
New Hampshire				
431916071125901	NH-BAW 10	Belknap	25.0	Stratified deposits, undifferentiated
434221071051501	NH-OXW 38	Carroll	114.7	Stratified deposits, undifferentiated
435948071220301	NH-ADW 14	Carroll	79.5	Stratified deposits, undifferentiated
435948071220302	NH-ADW 15	Carroll	18	Stratified deposits, undifferentiated
425543072175801	NH-KEW 2	Cheshire	18.0	Outwash
442450071052301	NH-SJW 2	Coos	40.7	Outwash
442830071321001	NH-LCW 1	Coos	30.0	Stratified deposits, undifferentiated
444733071094901	NH-ETW 1	Coos	30.0	Outwash
445334071291701	NH-CTW 73	Coos	27	Stratified deposits, undifferentiated
433616072074001	NH-ENW 30	Grafton	37.5	Stratified deposits, undifferentiated
434952071390901	NH-CBW 34	Grafton	106.6	Stratified deposits, undifferentiated
441401071531501	NH-LLW 19	Grafton	42.	Stratified deposits, undifferentiated
424800071295301	NH-NAW 218	Hillsborough	42.5	Delta drift
425744071532001	NH-GSW 75	Hillsborough	68.0	Stratified deposits, undifferentiated
430235071275501	NH-HTW 5	Merrimack	103	Crystalline rocks, noncarbonate
431034071340501	NH-CVW 312	Merrimack	480	Bedrock
431049071324301	NH-CVW 4	Merrimack	40.7	Lacustrine deposits
431120071284201	NH-PBW 148	Merrimack	94	Bedrock
431224071303601	NH-CVW 2	Merrimack	60.0	Stratified deposits, undifferentiated
431540071452801	NH-WCW 1	Merrimack	43.0	Outwash
432343071570901	NH-NLW 1	Merrimack	21.0	Till
432428071390701	NH-FKW 1	Merrimack	52	Outwash
430212070505201	NH-GTW 141	Rockingham	405.0	Bedrock
430409071010101	NH-EPW 90	Rockingham	37.	Stratified deposits, undifferentiated
430527071140101	NH-DDW 46	Rockingham	47.5	Stratified deposits, undifferentiated
430721071005001	NH-LIW 1	Strafford	32.8	Stratified deposits, undifferentiated
432534071095601	NH-NFW 53	Strafford	60.	Stratified deposits, undifferentiated
432322072112401	NH-NPW 3	Sullivan	57	Stratified deposits, undifferentiated
432322072112402	NH-NPW 6	Sullivan	20	Stratified deposits, undifferentiated
Vermont				
440016073070901	VT-MGW 11	Addison		
424810073160401	VT-PQW 1	Bennington	17.8	Stratified deposits, undifferentiated
443646073124901	VT-MJW 3	Chittenden	40.0	Stratified deposits, undifferentiated
444731071514701	VT-BIW 1	Essex	35.0	Stratified deposits, undifferentiated
443405072323501	VT-MPW 1	Lamoille	50.0	Stratified deposits, undifferentiated
435343072151801	VT-WOW 1	Orange	54.0	Stratified deposits, undifferentiated
443952072114001	VT-GLW 1	Orleans	82.0	Stratified deposits, undifferentiated
434217073010601	VT-PFW 8	Rutland	42.0	Stratified deposits, undifferentiated
441215072483101	VT-WAW 2	Washington	45.5	Stratified deposits, undifferentiated
431551072350601	VT-CKW 1	Windsor	22.0	Stratified deposits, undifferentiated
433240072242901	VT-HLW 54	Windsor	51.0	Stratified deposits, undifferentiated
435129072483301	VT-RJW 1	Windsor	73.0	Stratified deposits, undifferentiated

Surface-Water Streamflow

Computed annual runoff for the 2011 water year was the sixth highest on record for New Hampshire and the highest on record for Vermont (fig. 3; U.S. Geological Survey, 2011a). The ranking is based on a 111-year reference period (water years 1901 to 2011). The 2011 annual runoff, in general, was greater than the 90th percentile of the reference period for New Hampshire and Vermont; some hydrologic cataloging units in the Connecticut and St. Lawrence River Basins had the highest recorded annual runoffs (fig. 4; U.S. Geological Survey, 2011b). Annual runoff in the Piscataqua River Basin in southern New Hampshire was generally in the normal range.

Streamflow data for 11 representative streamgages used as indicators of monthly runoff across both States are provided in figures 5 to 15 (in back of report). Daily mean streamflow for water year 2011 is shown in relation to historical maximum, minimum, and mean streamflows, and annual mean streamflow for the period of record is shown in relation to the 25th, 50th, and 75th percentiles. Annual mean streamflows less than the 25th percentile are to be considered below normal; between the 25th and 75th percentile, normal; and above the 75th percentile, above normal. Hydrographs of monthly flow for the 11 representative streamgages are available on the Internet at http://nh.water.usgs.gov/WaterData/curr htm.

Androscoggin River Basin

Annual runoff for the Androscoggin River Basin was recorded at four streamgages. Annual runoff was above normal and generally in the greater than 90th-percentile class (fig. 4). For example, annual mean streamflow for the Diamond River near Wentworth Location, N.H. (01052500), of 478 cubic feet per second (ft^3/s) is the fifth highest on record (fig. 5, in back of report) and is 134 percent of the period of record annual mean of 358 ft^3/s.

Saco River Basin

Annual runoff for the Saco River Basin was recorded at four streamgages. Annual runoff was above normal and generally in the greater than 90th-percentile class (fig. 4). For example, annual mean streamflow for the Saco River near Conway, N.H. (01064500), of 1,422 ft^3/s is the fourth highest on record (fig. 6, in back of report) and is 147 percent of the period of record annual mean of 967 ft^3/s.

Piscataqua River Basin

Annual runoff for the Piscataqua River Basin was recorded at eight streamgages. Annual runoff was normal (fig. 4). For example, annual mean streamflow for the Lamprey River near Newmarket, N.H. (01073500), of 289 ft^3/s is the 40th highest on record (fig. 7, in back of report) and is 99 percent of the period of record annual mean of 292 ft^3/s.

Merrimack River Basin

Annual runoff for the Merrimack River Basin was recorded at 21 streamgages. Annual runoff was generally above normal and greater than the 90th percentile in northern parts of the basin (fig. 4). For example, annual mean streamflow for the Pemigewasset River at Plymouth, N.H. (01076500), of 2,207 ft^3/s is the second highest on record (fig. 8, in back of report) and is 159 percent of the period of record annual mean of 1,389 ft^3/s. The annual mean streamflow for the Merrimack River near Goffs Falls, below Manchester, N.H. (01092000), of 7,067 ft^3/s is the 10th highest on record (fig. 9, in back of report) and is about 129 percent of the period of record annual mean of 5,486 ft^3/s.

Connecticut River Basin

Annual runoff for the Connecticut River Basin was recorded at 29 streamgages. Annual runoff was generally greater than the 90th percentile; some subbasins in Vermont had the highest annual runoff on record (fig. 4). For example, annual mean streamflow for the Ammonoosuc River at Bethlehem Junction, N.H. (01137500), of 309 ft^3/s is the third highest on record (fig. 10, in back of report) and is about 144 percent of the period of record annual mean of 214 ft^3/s. The annual mean streamflow for the White River at West Hartford, Vt. (01144000), of 2,258 ft^3/s is the highest on record (fig. 11, in back of report) and is about 183 percent of the period of record annual mean of 1,231 ft^3/s.

Hudson River Basin

Annual runoff for the Hudson River Basin was recorded at one streamgage. Annual runoff was generally greater than the 90th percentile (fig. 4). Annual mean streamflow for the Walloomsac River near North Bennington, Vt. (01334000), of 340 ft^3/s is the second highest on record (fig. 12, in back of report) and is 150 percent of the period of record annual mean of 226 ft^3/s.

St. Lawrence River Basin

Annual runoff for the St. Lawrence River Basin was recorded at 41streamgages. Annual runoff was generally greater than the 90th percentile; some subbasins had the highest annual runoff on record (fig. 4). For example, annual mean streamflows for Otter Creek at Middlebury, Vt. (04282500), Dog River at Northfield Falls, Vt. (04287000), and Missisquoi River near East Berkshire, Vt. (04293500), were the highest on record (figs. 13–15, in back of report) and were 184, 195, and 165 percent, respectively, of the period of record annual mean streamflows.

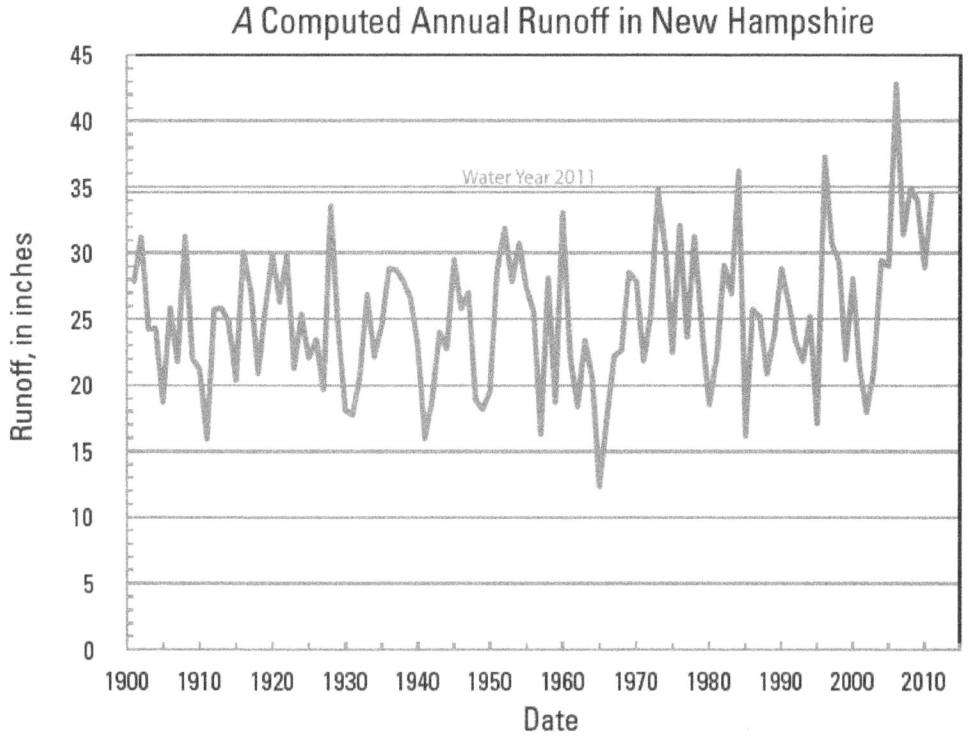

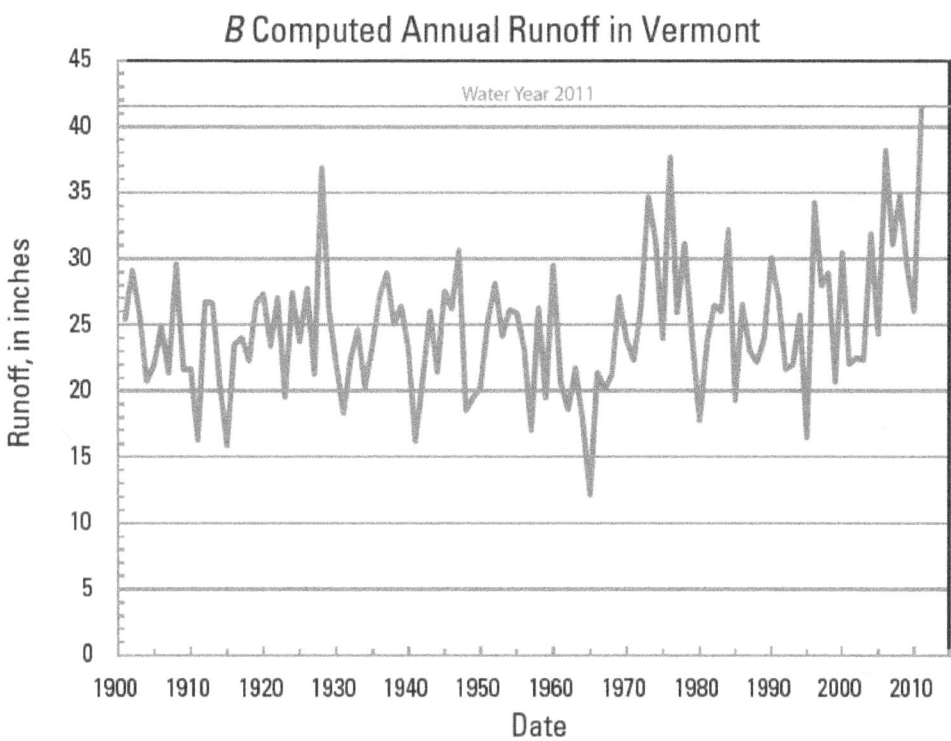

Figure 3.   Computed annual runoff in *A,* New Hampshire and *B,* Vermont for 1901 to 2011. (From U.S. Geological Survey, 2011a).

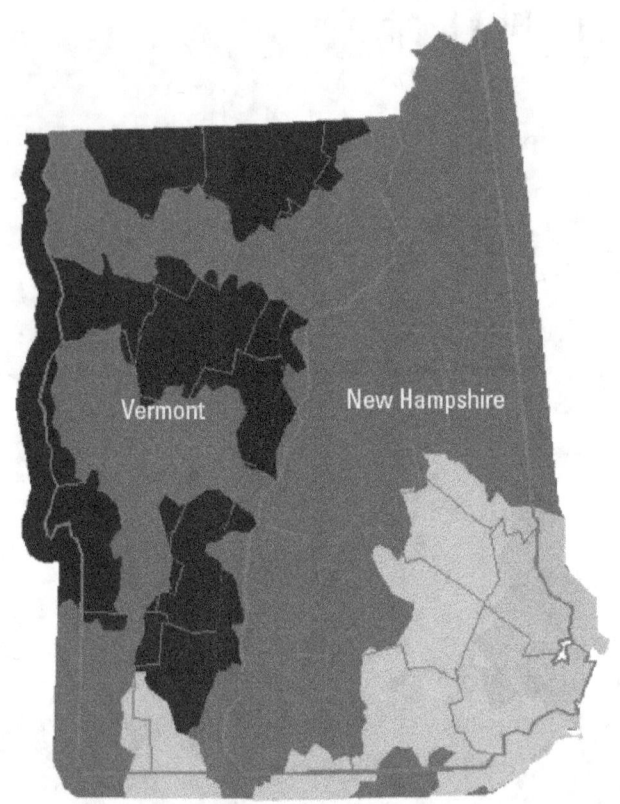

EXPLANATION
Annual runoff, in percentile classes

Lowest	< 10	10 - 24	25 - 75	76 - 90	>90	Highest	No data

Figure 4. Annual runoff for water year 2011, as a percentile of historical streamflow, by hydrologic cataloging units (HUC8) in New Hampshire and Vermont. (From U.S. Geological Survey, 2011b; <, less than; >, greater than).

Reservoir and Lake Elevations

The total combined usable storage of five major reservoirs in both States is 22,436 million cubic feet (ft^3). Variations in month-end average usable capacity for the five major reservoirs are shown in figure 16. At the beginning of the water year, the actual usable storage from these reservoirs was 15,703 million ft^3 or 70 percent of capacity. Average reservoir storage rose to 86 percent of capacity through October and was followed by a generally steady seasonal decline to a minimum capacity of 52 percent by the end of February, water year 2011. Average reservoir storage increased to a maximum of 96 percent through April and then generally declined. Month-end capacities for the five major reservoirs are available on the Internet at http://nh.water.usgs.gov/WaterData/curr htm.

Lake Champlain daily mean elevations for water year 2011 and daily maximum, minimum, and average elevations for water years 1940 to 2010 are shown in figure 17. The annual mean elevation for water year 2011 was the highest for the period of record. All daily mean elevations for water year 2011 were greater than historical average daily mean elevations. Daily mean elevations in April, May, June, and September were greater than historical maximum daily mean elevations.

Groundwater Levels

The groundwater observation well network included 41 wells—29 wells in New Hampshire and 12 wells in Vermont (table 2). Well locations are shown in figure 2 and are referenced by local well name (table 2). Month-end conditions are characterized in table 3 for the 38 wells with more than 10 years of data. Water levels less than the 25th percentile are characterized as below normal, from the 25th to the 75th percentile as normal, and above the 75th percentile as above normal.

Groundwater levels in New Hampshire were generally normal (table 3); however, many wells, such as NH–WCW 1 (fig. 18), had above-normal levels for April, May, and September, coincident with flooding events. Groundwater levels in Vermont were generally normal to above normal. Most of the wells had above-normal levels for October, November, April, May, June, August, and September. Further information on groundwater conditions and the groundwater observation well network is available on the Internet at http://groundwater-watch.usgs.gov/NHV/StateMaps/NH.html.

Floods

Record flooding occurred in April, May, and August of water year 2011. Peak-of-record streamflows occurred at 25 streamgages with more than 10 years of record. Flooding in April 2011 was widespread in parts of northern New Hampshire and Vermont. Flash flooding in May 2011 was isolated to central and northeastern Vermont. Devastating flooding in August 2011 occurred throughout most of Vermont and in parts of New Hampshire as the result of the heavy rains associated with Tropical Storm Irene.

To gain a historical perspective on the relative magnitude of flood events in water year 2011, peak streamflows were ranked against previously recorded peaks of record (table 4). In water year 2011, many rivers in New Hampshire and Vermont reached historic levels. For example, the April 2011 flood of the Lamoille River at East Georgia, Vt. (04292500), produced the largest streamflow in the 82-year period of record, whereas the August 2011 flood of the White River at West Hartford, Vt. (01144000), produced the largest streamflow since 1927 (table 4).

Annual peak streamflows recorded at streamgages during each flood event are shown relative to the contributing drainage area in figure 19. To gain perspective on the relative magnitude of the flood peaks, envelope lines for regional maximum flood streamflows (Crippen and Bue, 1977) and for maximum recorded flood streamflows in and adjacent to New Hampshire, as well as a regression line relating the 100-year (Q_{100}) streamflow to drainage area (Olson, 2008), have been included in figure 19.

Flood of April 26–29, 2011

The winter of 2010–11 produced an abnormally high snowpack in both New Hampshire and Vermont. In Burlington, Vt., the third highest total snowfall (128 in.) was recorded since records were established in 1893 (National Weather Service, 2011). This snowpack in conjunction with record rainfall in the months of April and May produced severe, widespread flooding in large basins within both States. The heaviest rainfall and resulting riverine flooding occurred April 26–29, 2011, across the Androscoggin, Connecticut, and St. Lawrence River Basins in northern New Hampshire and Vermont. The water level in Lake Champlain surpassed prior historical records and crested at 103.27 ft on May 6, 2011. Annual peak streamflows for water year 2011 were recorded at 29 streamgages (table 4). Peak-of-record streamflows were recorded at nine streamgages in the Connecticut and St. Lawrence River Basins.

Five streamgages in New Hampshire recorded stages at or above the flood stages designated by the National Weather Service. Minor to moderate flooding was reported in the Androscoggin, Pemigewasset, and the Connecticut River Basins. Flooding in Vermont was more widespread; 10 streamgages or lake gages recorded stages at or above the flood stages designated by the National Weather Service. Minor to moderate flooding occurred in the Passumpsic, Otter Creek, and Winooski River Basins. Major flooding occurred in the Lamoille and Missisquoi River Basins, and at Lake Champlain.

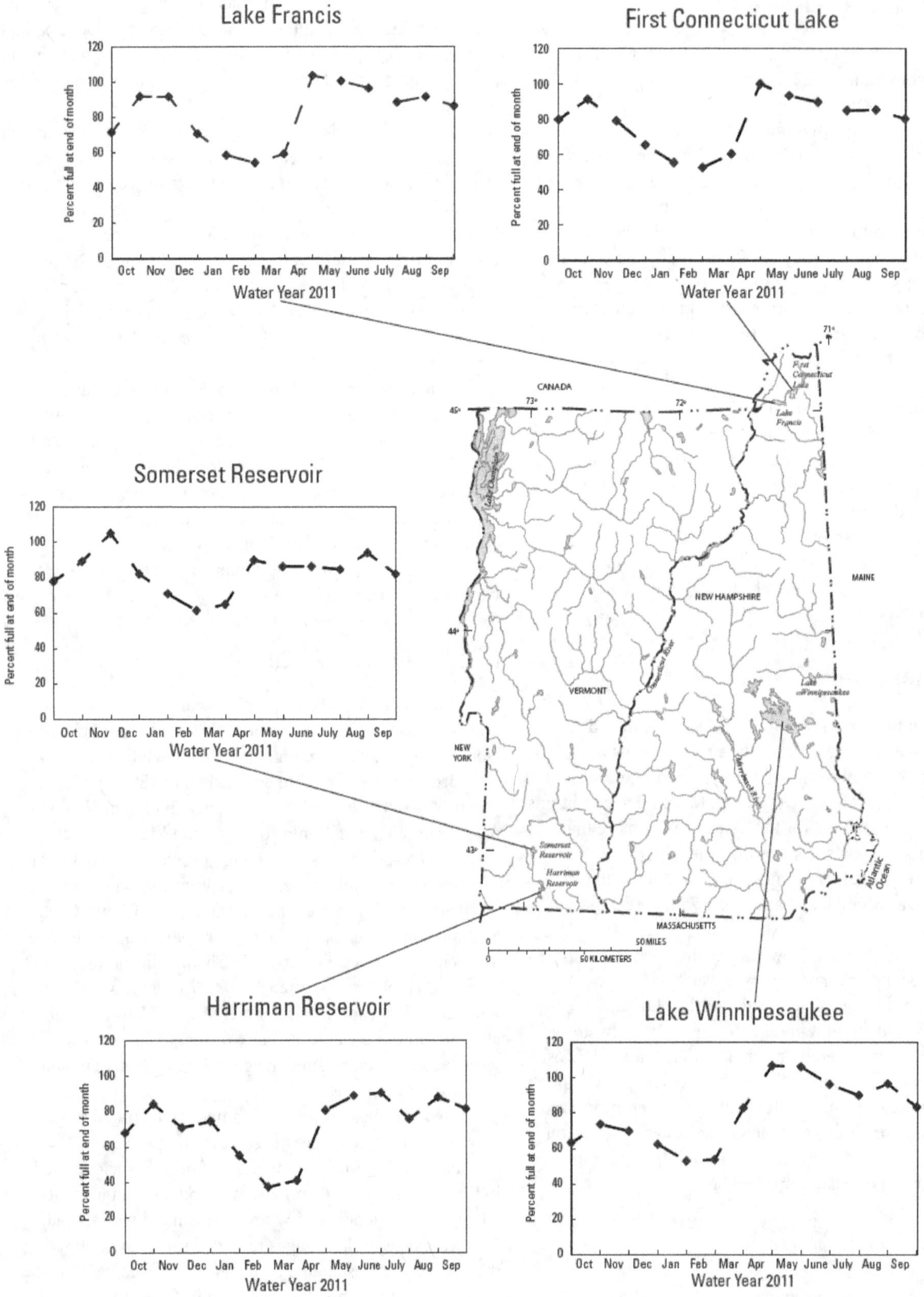

Figure 16.   Locations of selected lakes or reservoirs in New Hampshire and Vermont and corresponding month-end contents, water year 2011.

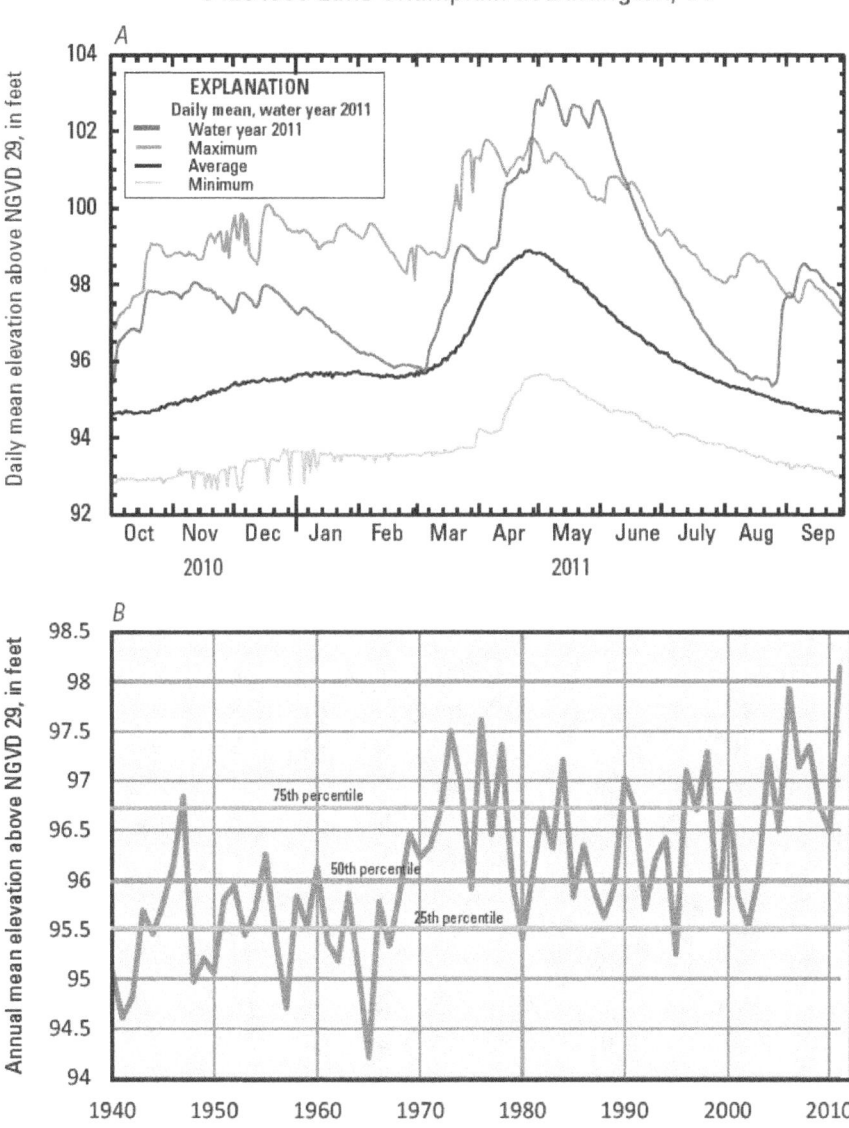

Figure 17. *A,* Daily mean surface-water elevation at station 04294500 Lake Champlain at Burlington, Vermont, water year 2011, and daily maximum, minimum, and average elevations for water years 1940–2010 and *B,* annual mean elevations for water years 1940–2011, and the 25th, 50th, and 75th percentiles.

Table 3.   Month-end groundwater-level conditions for 38 wells in New Hampshire and Vermont, water year 2011.

[Month-end groundwater levels were measured in 38 long-term wells completed in unconsolidated material. Conditions are in relation to the period of record for each well. Conditions: N, normal, within the 25th to 75th percentile range of record for the month; -, below normal, within the lowest 25th percentile of record for the month; +, above normal, within the highest 25th percentile of record for the month. See figure 2 for well locations. Prefixes NH and VT have been omitted from the well names. NH, New Hampshire; VT, Vermont; --, no data]

NH groundwater wells (Town)	COUNTY	OCT	NOV	DEC	JAN	FEB	MAR	APR	MAY	JUNE	JULY	AUG	SEP
BAW-10 (BARNSTEAD)	Belknap	N	N	-	N	N	N	N	N	N	N	N	-
ADW-14 (ALBANY)	Carroll	N	N	+	-	-	N	+	+	N	-	N	+
ADW-15 (ALBANY)	Carroll	N	N	+	-	-	N	+	+	N	-	N	+
OXW-38 (OSSIPEE)	Carroll	N	N	N	N	N	N	+	N	N	N	N	+
KEW-2 (KEENE)	Cheshire	+	N	N	+	+	N	+	+	+	+	+	+
CTW-73 (COLEBROOK)	Coos	N	N	N	N	N	N	N	N	N	N	N	N
ETW-1 (ERROL)	Coos	N	N	-	-	-	N	-	N	-	N	N	N
LCW-1 (LANCASTER)	Coos	--	N	N	+	--	N	+	N	--	N	--	--
SJW-2 (SHELBURNE)	Coos	-	N	N	-	N	N	-	N	-	-	-	-
CBW-34 (CAMPTON)	Grafton	N	N	N	-	-	+	+	+	N	-	N	+
ENW-30 (ENFIELD)	Grafton	N	N	N	N	--	--	+	N	N	--	--	-
LLW-19 (LISBON)	Grafton	N	N	N	+	+	+	N	+	N	-	-	+
GSW-75 (GREENFIELD)	Hillsborough	N	N	N	-	-	N	N	-	N	N	N	N
NAW-218 (NASHUA)	Hillsborough	N	N	N	N	N	+	N	N	N	N	N	N
CVW-2 (CONCORD)	Merrimack	+	+	+	+	+	+	+	+	+	+	+	+
CVW-4 (CONCORD)	Merrimack	-	-	N	-	-	N	N	N	N	N	N	+
FKW-1 (FRANKLIN)	Merrimack	-	-	-	-	-	N	N	N	N	N	N	+
HTW-5 (HOOKSETT)	Merrimack	-	-	-	-	-	+	N	N	N	N	N	+
NLW-1 (NEW LONDON)	Merrimack	N	+	+	N	N	+	+	+	+	+	+	+
WCW-1 (WARNER)	Merrimack	N	N	N	N	N	+	--	--	+	--	+	+
DDW-46 (DEERFIELD)	Rockingham	-	-	N	-	-	N	N	+	N	N	N	N
EPW 90 (EPPING)	Rockingham	--	--	--	--	--	--	--	--	--	--	--	--
LIW-1 (LEE)	Strafford	N	+	+	N	--	--	+	+	+	--	--	--
NFW-53 (NEW DURHAM)	Strafford	N	N	+	N	N	+	N	+	N	+	N	+
NPW-3 (NEWPORT)	Sullivan	N	N	N	-	-	+	N	+	N	-	N	+
NPW-6 (NEWPORT)	Sullivan	N	N	N	-	-	N	N	N	N	-	N	+

VT groundwater wells (Town)	COUNTY	OCT	NOV	DEC	JAN	FEB	MAR	APR	MAY	JUNE	JULY	AUG	SEP
MGW-11 (MIDDLEBURY)	Addison	+	N	-	N	N	N	N	N	N	N	+	+
PQW-1 (POWNAL)	Bennington	+	+	+	N	N	+	+	+	N	N	+	+
MJW-3 (MILTON)	Chittenden	+	+	+	+	+	+	+	+	+	--	+	+
BIW-1 (BRIGHTON)	Essex	+	+	+	+	+	+	+	+	+	+	N	-
MPW-1 (MORRISTOWN)	Lamoille	+	+	N	N	N	N	+	+	+	+	+	+
WOW-1 (WEST FAIRLEE)	Orange	+	+	+	N	N	N	+	+	+	N	+	+
GLW-1 (GLOVER)	Orleans	+	+	+	+	+	N	+	+	+	N	+	+
PFW-8 (PITTSFORD)	Rutland	+	+	+	+	+	+	+	+	+	+	+	+
WAW-2 (WAITSFIELD)	Washington	+	N	N	N	N	N	+	+	+	N	+	+
CKW-1 (CHESTER)	Windsor	+	+	+	-	-	N	+	+	+	N	+	+
HLW-54 (HARTLAND)	Windsor	N	N	N	N	N	N	+	+	N	N	+	+
RJW-1 (ROCHESTER)	Windsor	+	N	N	N	N	N	N	N	+	N	--	+

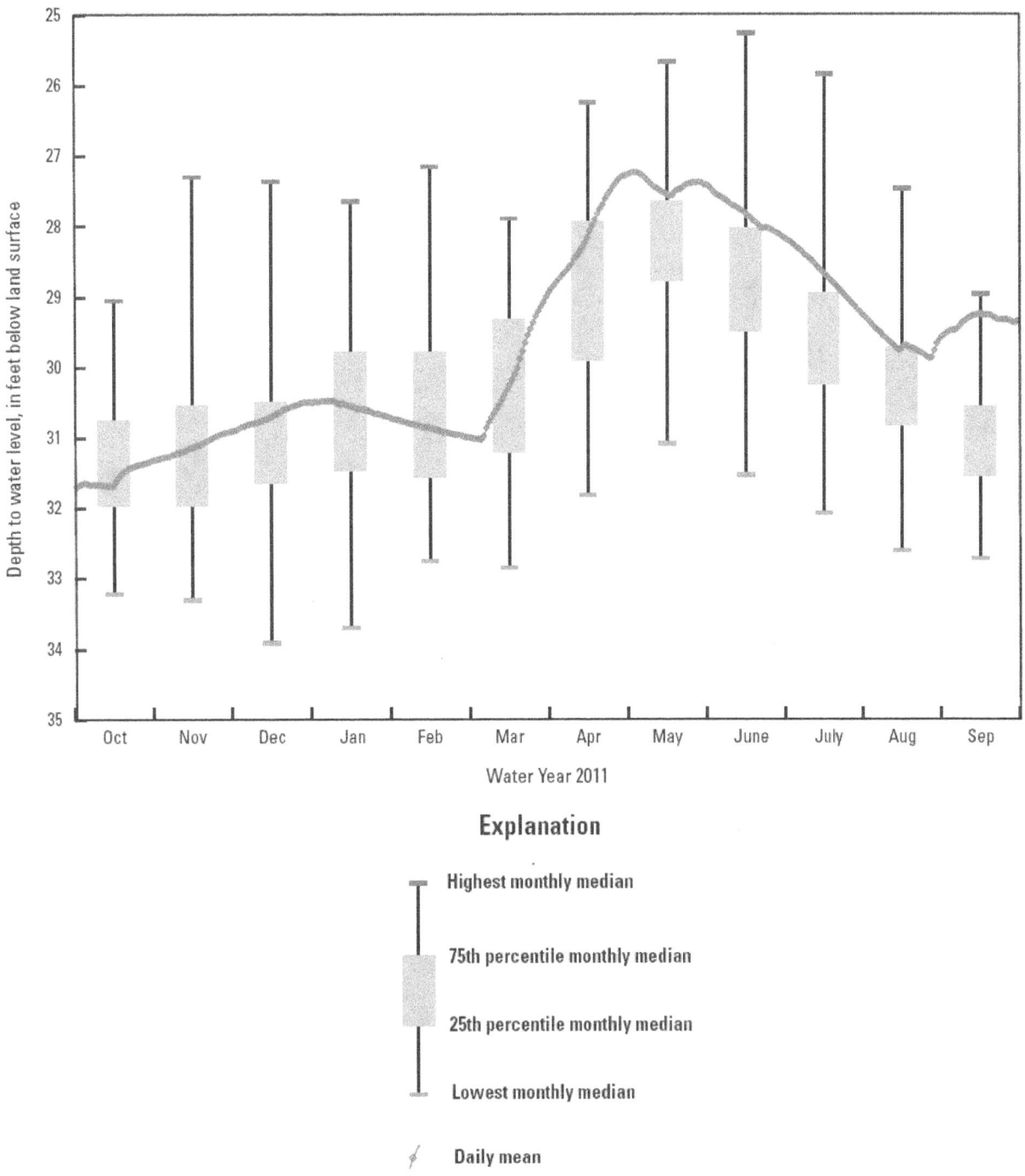

Figure 18. Daily mean depths to water in groundwater well 431500714528011, NH-WCW1, Town of Warner, New Hampshire, water year 2011, in relation to the distribution of monthly mean depths to water, water years 1965–2010.

Table 4. Peak stages and streamflows for selected New Hampshire and Vermont streamgages during record flooding in April, May, and August, water year 2011, and historical peak streamflows.

[mi², square miles; ft, foot; ft³/s, cubic feet per second; NH, New Hampshire; VT, Vermont]

Station number	Station name	Drainage area (mi²)	Annual data for Water Year 2011				Historical data		
			Date	Peak stage (ft)	Peak streamflow (ft³/s)	Rank[a]	Number of years	Year	Peak streamflow (ft³/s)
Flood of April 26–29, 2011									
Androscoggin River Basin									
01052500	DIAMOND RIVER NEAR WENTWORTH LOCATION, NH	152	4/27/2011	10.03	7,780	9	70	1998	12,800
Connecticut River Basin									
01129200	CONNECTICUT R BELOW INDIAN STREAM NR PITTSBURG, NH	254	4/27/2011	8.85	6,550	1	55	2011	6,550
01129420	CAPON BROOK AT VT 102, NEAR CANAAN, VT	4.71	4/27/2011	10.67	423	1	5	2011	423
01129500	CONNECTICUT RIVER AT NORTH STRATFORD, NH	799	4/27/2011	14.90	29,500	2	81	1998	32,300
01130000	UPPER AMMONOOSUC RIVER NEAR GROVETON, NH	232	4/28/2011	7.52	6,940	12	65	1969	24,100
01131500	CONNECTICUT RIVER NEAR DALTON, NH	1,514	4/29/2011	22.07	33,200	8	84	1936	48,300
01138500	CONNECTICUT RIVER AT WELLS RIVER, VT	2,644	4/29/2011	13.58	47,200	6	62	1973	57,100
St. Lawrence River Basin									
04282700	LEWIS CREEK TRIBUTARY AT STARKSBORO, VT	5.31	4/27/2011	23.34	598	4	25	1974	1,350
04282780	LEWIS CREEK AT NORTH FERRISBURG, VT.	77.2	4/27/2011	6.04	4,690	1	22	2011	4,690
04282795	LAPLATTE RIVER AT SHELBURNE FALLS, VT.	44.6	4/27/2011	6.82	2,120	3	22	1996	2,640
04282813	POTASH BR @ QUEEN CITY PARK RD, NR BURLINGTON, VT	7.18	4/27/2011	5.34	634	1	7	2011	634
04288225	W BRANCH LITTLE R ABV BINGHAM FALLS NEAR STOWE, VT	4.67	4/27/2011	4.92	1,430	2	11	2010	1,740
04288230	RANCH BROOK AT RANCH CAMP, NEAR STOWE, VT	3.80	4/27/2011	4.47	983	2	11	2010	1,130
04288400	BRYANT BROOK AT WATERBURY CENTER, VT	2.64	4/27/2011	12.98	223	3	25	1973	302
04289000	LITTLE RIVER NEAR WATERBURY, VT	111	4/27/2011	16.35	5,240	2	76	1936	6,520
04289600	WINOOSKI RIVER TRIBUTARY NEAR RICHMOND, VT	0.71	4/27/2011	14.28	85	2	24	1972	102
04290335	ALLEN BROOK AT VT 2A, NEAR ESSEX JUNCTION, VT	9.9	4/27/2011	6.42	2,350	1	6	2011	2,350
04290700	BAILEY BROOK AT EAST HARDWICK, VT	2.52	4/27/2011	14.57	219	3	28	1973	285
04292000	LAMOILLE RIVER AT JOHNSON, VT	310	4/27/2011	16.97	13,800	3	85	1995	19,000
04292100	STONY BROOK NEAR EDEN, VT	4.21	4/27/2011	13.38	611	3	23	1973	890
04292500	LAMOILLE RIVER AT EAST GEORGIA, VT	686	4/27/2011	13.10	28,800	1	82	2011	28,800
04292770	STEVENS BROOK AT LEMNAH DRIVE, AT ST ALBANS, VT	1.54	4/26/2011	3.54	297	1	5	2011	297
04292810	JEWETT BROOK AT VT 38, NEAR ST. ALBANS, VT	3.74	4/28/2011	6.74	416	1	3	2011	416
04293800	MISSISQUOI RIVER TRIBUTARY AT SHELDON JUNCTION, VT	1.69	4/27/2011	14.84	104	3	29	2002	122
04293900	HUNGERFORD BR @ HIGHGATE RD NR HIGHGATE CENTER, VT	18.6	4/27/2011	6.02	1,360	1	2	2011	1,360

Table 4. Peak stages and streamflows for selected New Hampshire and Vermont streamgages during record flooding in April, May, and August, water year 2011, and historical peak streamflows.—Continued

[mi², square miles; ft, foot; ft³/s, cubic feet per second; NH, New Hampshire; VT, Vermont]

Station number	Station name	Drainage area (mi²)	Annual data for Water Year 2011				Historical data		
			Date	Peak stage (ft)	Peak streamflow (ft³/s)	Rank[a]	Number of years	Year	Peak streamflow (ft³/s)
	Flood of April 26–29, 2011—Continued								
	St. Lawrence River Basin—Continued								
04294000	MISSISQUOI RIVER AT SWANTON, VT	850	4/28/2011	7.49	25,500	6	22	1996	37,700
04294300	PIKE RIVER AT EAST FRANKLIN, NR ENOSBURG FALLS, VT	34.5	4/27/2011	6.23	2,400	2	10	2006	3,010
04296300	PHERRINS RIVER TRIBUTARY NEAR ISLAND POND, VT	1.05	4/27/2011	12.78	80	3	28	1969	140
04296500	CLYDE RIVER AT NEWPORT, VT	142	4/28/2011	9.37	3,820	2	95	1936	3,900
	Flood of May 27, 2011								
	Connecticut River Basin								
01134800	KIRBY BROOK AT CONCORD, VT	8.05	5/27/2011	17.57	1,640	1	24	2011	1,640
01135150	POPE BROOK (SITE W-3) NEAR NORTH DANVILLE, VT	3.25	5/27/2011	5.34	549	1	21	2011	549
01135300	SLEEPERS RIVER (SITE W-5) NEAR ST. JOHNSBURY, VT	42.9	5/27/2011	8.56	9,360	1	21	2011	9,360
01135500	PASSUMPSIC RIVER AT PASSUMPSIC, VT	436	5/27/2011	18.92	13,800	4	84	1973	18,200
01135700	JOES BROOK TRIBUTARY NEAR EAST BARNET, VT	0.76	5/27/2011	18.63	324	1	23	2011	324
	St. Lawrence River Basin								
04292355	MORGAN BR TRIB AT OLD NO 11 RD, NEAR WESTFORD, VT	2.15	5/27/2011	12.23	292	1	5	2011	292
	Flood of August 28–September 2, 2011								
	Saco River Basin								
010642505	SACO RIVER AT RIVER STREET, AT BARTLETT, NH	91	8/28/2011	14.83	29,100	1	2	2011	29,100
01064500	SACO RIVER NEAR CONWAY, NH	385	8/28/2011	17.23	58,200	1	88	2011	58,200
01064801	BEARCAMP RIVER AT SOUTH TAMWORTH, NH	67.6	8/28/2011	9.35	5,640	2	19	1998	6,150
	Merrimack River Basin								
01074520	EAST BRANCH PEMIGEWASSET RIVER AT LINCOLN, NH	115	8/28/2011	17.50	29,300	1	19	2011	29,300
01075000	PEMIGEWASSET RIVER AT WOODSTOCK, NH	193	8/28/2011	16.97	53,700	1	67	2011	53,700
01076000	BAKER RIVER NEAR RUMNEY, NH	143	8/28/2011	13.99	11,300	9	77	1927	25,900
01076500	PEMIGEWASSET RIVER AT PLYMOUTH, NH	622	8/29/2011	21.38	41,100	9	108	1936	65,400
01077400	COCKERMOUTH RIVER BELOW HARDY BROOK, AT GROTON, NH	21.4	8/28/2011	11.17	5,260	1	3	2011	5,260

Table 4. Peak stages and streamflows for selected New Hampshire and Vermont streamgages during record flooding in April, May, and August, water year 2011, and historical peak streamflows.—Continued

[mi², square miles; ft, foot; ft³/s, cubic feet per second; NH, New Hampshire; VT, Vermont]

Station number	Station name	Drainage area (mi²)	Annual data for Water Year 2011				Historical data		
			Date	Peak stage (ft)	Peak streamflow (ft³/s)	Rank[a]	Number of years	Year	Peak streamflow (ft³/s)
	Flood of August 28–September 2, 2011—Continued								
	Connecticut River Basin								
01133000	EAST BRANCH PASSUMPSIC RIVER NEAR EAST HAVEN, VT	53.8	8/28/2011	9.79	3,250	3	52	1973	4,450
01137500	AMMONOOSUC RIVER AT BETHLEHEM JUNCTION, NH	87.6	8/28/2011	10.90	8,600	6	72	1995	11,300
01139000	WELLS RIVER AT WELLS RIVER, VT	98.4	8/28/2011	9.03	5,170	2	71	1973	5,970
01139700	WAITS RIVER TRIBUTARY NEAR WEST TOPSHAM, VT	1.09	8/28/2011	11.95	146	1	22	2011	146
01139800	EAST ORANGE BRANCH AT EAST ORANGE, VT	8.95	8/28/2011	5.14	719	2	53	1990	800
01142400	THIRD BRANCH WHITE RIVER TRIBUTARY AT RANDOLPH, VT	0.77	8/28/2011	12.55	117	4	25	1998	327
01142500	AYERS BROOK AT RANDOLPH, VT	30.5	8/28/2011	15.04	3,920	1	72	2011	3,920
01144000	WHITE RIVER AT WEST HARTFORD, VT	690	8/29/2011	28.36	90,100	2	96	1927	120,000
01144500	CONNECTICUT RIVER AT WEST LEBANON, NH	4,092	8/29/2011	29.66	105,000	4	98	1927	136,000
01150800	KENT BROOK NEAR KILLINGTON, VT	3.31	8/28/2011	15.70	2,840	1	24	2011	2,840
01151200	OTTAUQUECHEE RIVET TRIBUTARY NEAR QUECHEE, VT	0.82	8/28/2011	11.73	59	2	22	1973	93
01153300	MIDDLE BRANCH WILLIAMS RIVER TRIBUTARY AT CHESTER, VT	3.16	8/28/2011	21.65	602	1	26	2011	602
01153550	WILLIAMS RIVER NEAR ROCKINGHAM VT	112	8/28/2011	17.94	21,300	1	25	2011	21,300
01154000	SAXTONS RIVER AT SAXTONS RIVER, VT	72.2	8/28/2011	19.58	21,600	1	53	2011	21,600
01154500	CONNECTICUT RIVER AT NORTH WALPOLE, NH	5,493	8/29/2011	31.38	99,700	1	70	2011	99,700
01156300	WHETSTONE BROOK TRIBUTARY NEAR MARLBORO, VT	1.05	8/28/2011	22.36	762	1	24	2011	762
01157000	ASHUELOT RIVER NEAR GILSUM, NH	71.1	8/28/2011	8.18	2,300	13	62	2006	10,200
	Hudson River Basin								
01334000	WALLOOMSAC RIVER NEAR NORTH BENNINGTON, VT	111	8/28/2011	12.82	9,420	1	80	2011	9,420
	St. Lawrence River Basin								
04280000	POULTNEY RIVER BELOW FAIR HAVEN, VT	187	8/29/2011	23.28	12,800	2	83	1945	14,800
04280240	METTAWEE RIVER TRIBUTARY NO. 3 AT VT 30, AT EAST RUPERT, VT	2.59	8/28/2011	15.01	220	1	5	2011	220
04282000	OTTER CREEK AT CENTER RUTLAND, VT	307	8/29/2011	17.43	15,700	1	83	2011	15,700
04282300	BRANDY BROOK AT BREAD LOAF, VT	2.24	8/28/2011	12.84	306	3	27	2000	546
04282500	OTTER CREEK AT MIDDLEBURY, VT	628	9/2/2011	7.34	6,180	15	96	1927	13,600
04282525	NEW HAVEN RIVER @ BROOKSVILLE, NR MIDDLEBURY, VT	115	8/28/2011	12.95	16,700	2	21	1998	21,700
04286000	WINOOSKI RIVER AT MONTPELIER, VT	397	8/28/2011	19.05	14,600	4	96	1927	57,000

Table 4. Peak stages and streamflows for selected New Hampshire and Vermont streamgages during record flooding in April, May, and August, water year 2011, and historical peak streamflows.—Continued

[mi², square miles; ft, foot; ft³/s, cubic feet per second; NH, New Hampshire; VT, Vermont]

Station number	Station name	Drainage area (mi²)	Annual data for Water Year 2011				Historical data		
			Date	Peak stage (ft)	Peak streamflow (ft³/s)	Rank[a]	Number of years	Year	Peak streamflow (ft³/s)
Flood of August 28–September 2, 2011—Continued									
St. Lawrence River Basin—Continued									
04287000	DOG RIVER AT NORTHFIELD FALLS, VT	76.1	8/28/2011	17.26	22,200	1	77	2011	22,200
04287300	SUNNY BROOK NEAR MONTPELIER, VT	2.31	8/28/2011	7.71	317	4	24	1973	342
04288000	MAD RIVER NEAR MORETOWN, VT	139	8/28/2011	19.26	24,200	1	84	2011	24,200
04290500	WINOOSKI RIVER NEAR ESSEX JUNCTION, VT	1,044	8/29/2011	22.18	35,000	3	84	1927	113,000
04293000	MISSISQUOI RIVER NEAR NORTH TROY, VT	131	8/29/2011	13.93	10,900	2	80	2002	11,500
04293005	DUNN BROOK AT VT 100, NEAR NEWPORT CENTER, VT	2.85	8/28/2011	18.33	574	1	5	2011	574
04293200	MUD CREEK AT BEAR MOUNTAIN RD, NEAR NORTH TROY, VT	37.1	8/28/2011	8.19	3,240	1	2	2011	3,240
04293430	NORTH BRANCH ABOVE RIVER STREET, AT RICHFORD, VT	64.8	8/29/2011	13.66	3,000	1	2	2011	3,000
04293500	MISSISQUOI RIVER NEAR EAST BERKSHIRE, VT	479	8/29/2011	14.12	14,700	9	95	1927	45,000
04293600	TROUT RIVER AT HOPKINS BR, NR ENOSBURG FALLS, VT	78.6	8/28/2011	15.96	10,500	1	2	2011	10,500
04296000	BLACK RIVER AT COVENTRY, VT	122	8/29/2011	8.20	4,070	1	60	2011	4,070
04296150	LORD BROOK NEAR EVANSVILLE, VT	4.76	8/28/2011	15.54	429	1	28	2011	429

[a]Rank of the maximum instantaneous peak streamflow measured during water year 2011 compared to historic annual peaks.

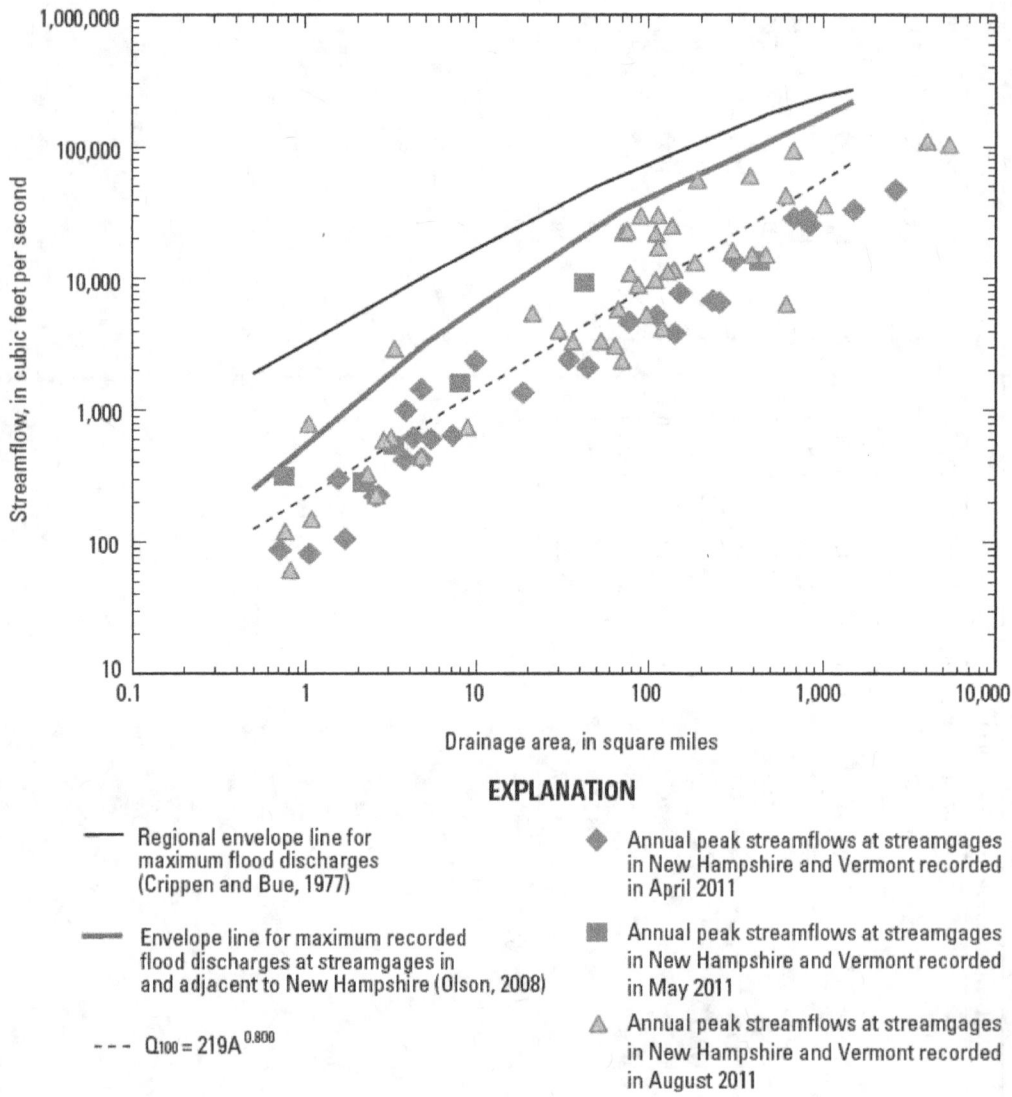

EXPLANATION

—— Regional envelope line for maximum flood discharges (Crippen and Bue, 1977)

—— Envelope line for maximum recorded flood discharges at streamgages in and adjacent to New Hampshire (Olson, 2008)

- - - $Q_{100} = 219A^{0.800}$

◆ Annual peak streamflows at streamgages in New Hampshire and Vermont recorded in April 2011

■ Annual peak streamflows at streamgages in New Hampshire and Vermont recorded in May 2011

△ Annual peak streamflows at streamgages in New Hampshire and Vermont recorded in August 2011

Figure 19. Annual peak streamflows at selected streamgages in New Hampshire and Vermont, water year 2011, in relation to the contributing drainage area, with envelope lines and a regression line relating the 100-year streamflow to drainage area (From Olson, 2008; Q_{100}, 100-year streamflow).

Flood of May 27, 2011

Flash flooding occurred on May 27, 2011, as a result of rainfall on already saturated soils. Localized riverine flooding occurred mainly in subbasins within the Connecticut River Basin in northeastern Vermont and was the result of severe thunderstorms and locally heavy rains of as much as 3 to 5 in. Annual peak streamflows for water year 2011 were recorded at six streamgages. Peak-of-record streamflows were recorded at five streamgages in the Connecticut and St. Lawrence River Basins (table 4).

Seven streamgages or lake gages recorded stages at or above the flood stages designated by the National Weather Service. Minor to moderate flooding occurred on the Androscoggin, Passumpsic, and Wells River Basins. Major flooding occurred in the Winooski River Basin and at Lake Champlain.

Lake Champlain

Record flooding occurred on Lake Champlain during the spring of 2011. Lake Champlain was above the National Weather Service flood stage of 100 ft for a 68-day period that spanned from April 13 to June 19, 2011 (fig. 17). Lake Champlain at Burlington, Vt. (04294500), was above the major flood level of 101.5 ft for 43 of the 68 days and peaked at 103.27 ft on May 6, 2011. This surpassed the maximum known elevation since at least 1827 of 102.1 ft, which occurred on May 4, 1869 (U.S. Geological Survey 2012).

Flood of August 28 to September 2, 2011

Widespread riverine flooding occurred August 28 to September 2, 2011, across the Saco, Merrimack, Connecticut, Hudson, and St. Lawrence River Basins as the result of heavy rains associated with Tropical Storm Irene. Rainfall ranged from 4 to 7 in. in less than 12 hours. Annual peak streamflows for water year 2011 were recorded at 53 streamgages. Peak-of-record streamflows were recorded at 24 streamgages in the Saco, Merrimack, Connecticut, Hudson, and St. Lawrence River Basins (table 4). Peak-of-record streamflows recorded at Kent Brook near Killington, Vt. (01150800), and Whetstone Brook Tributary near Marlboro, Vt. (01156300), resulted in runoff of 858 and 762 cubic feet per square mile, respectively, which were greater than the envelope line for maximum recorded flood streamflows at streamgages in and adjacent to New Hampshire (fig. 19).

Twelve streamgages in New Hampshire recorded stages at or above the flood stages designated by the National Weather Service. Minor to moderate flooding was reported in the Androscoggin, Saco, Baker, Smith, Warner, Suncook, and Ammonoosuc River Basins. Major flooding was reported in the Pemigewasset and the Connecticut River Basins. Eighteen streamgages in Vermont recorded stages at or above the flood stages designated by the National Weather Service. Minor to moderate flooding occurred in the Passumpsic, Poultney, and Black River Basins. Major flooding occurred in the Wells, Ayers, White, Williams, Walloomsac, Otter Creek, Winooski, Dog, Mad, Lamoille, and Missisquoi River Basins.

Summary

Record-high hydrologic conditions in New Hampshire and Vermont occurred during water year 2011 as characterized by 125 streamgages and lake gaging stations, 27 crest-stage gages, and 41 groundwater wells. This report summarizes hydrologic conditions in New Hampshire and Vermont for water year 2011 in terms of precipitation, streamflow, lake and reservoir elevations, and groundwater levels.

Computed annual runoff for water year 2011 was the sixth highest on record for New Hampshire and the highest on record for Vermont. Annual runoff was above normal and generally in the greater than 90th percentile in the Androscoggin, Saco, northern Merrimack, Connecticut, Hudson, and St. Lawrence River Basins. Annual runoff for some subbasins in the Connecticut and St. Lawrence River Basins was the highest ever recorded. In general, the Piscataquog River Basin experienced normal runoff in water year 2011.

At the beginning of the water year, the actual usable storage for First Connecticut Lake, Lake Francis, Somerset Reservoir, Harriman Reservoir, and Lake Winnipesaukee was 70 percent of capacity. Average storage for the five reservoirs rose to 86 percent of capacity through October and was followed by a generally steady seasonal decline to a minimum capacity of 52 percent by the end of February. Average reservoir storage increased to a maximum of 96 percent through April and then generally declined. Lake Champlain annual mean elevation for water year 2011 was the highest for the period of record. All daily mean elevations for water year 2011 were greater than historical average daily mean elevations. Daily mean elevations for periods in April, May, June, and September were greater than historical maximum daily mean elevations.

Groundwater levels were generally normal in New Hampshire and normal to above normal in Vermont. Many wells in New Hampshire recorded above normal levels for April, May, and September, coincident with flooding events. The majority of wells in Vermont recorded above-normal levels for October, November, April, May, June, August, and September.

Record flooding occurred in April, May, and August of water year 2011. Peak-of-record streamflows were recorded at 38 streamgages. Flooding in April 2011 was widespread in parts of northern New Hampshire and Vermont. Peak-of-record streamflows were recorded at nine streamgages. Flash flooding in May 2011 was isolated to central and northeastern Vermont. Peak-of-record streamflows were recorded at five streamgages. Record flooding occurred on Lake Champlain during the spring of 2011. Lake Champlain was above the National Weather Service flood stage for a 68-day period that spanned from April 13 to June 19, 2011. The peak elevation of 103.27 feet (ft) recorded on May 6, 2011, surpassed the maximum known elevation since at least 1827 of 102.1 ft. Devastating floods in August 2011 occurred throughout most of Vermont and in parts of New Hampshire as result of the heavy rains associated with Tropical Storm Irene. Rainfall ranged from 4 to 7 inches in less than 12 hours. Peak-of-record streamflows were recorded at 24 streamgages.

Acknowledgments

This report is the culmination of a concerted effort by dedicated personnel of the U.S. Geological Survey (USGS) who collected, processed, and compiled the data. The authors acknowledge the assistance provided by Robert Brown, Chandlee Keirstead, Glenn Berwick, Anthony Debonis, Heather Manzi, Kelsey-Ann Reagan, Celia Honigberg, and Cody Whelan in the collection of data. Thanks are extended to Philip Harte and Richard Verdi of the USGS for their technical reviews of this report.

References Cited

Crippen, J.R., and Bue, C.D., 1977, Maximum flood flows in the conterminous United States: U.S. Geological Survey Water-Supply Paper 1887, 52 p.

National Oceanic and Atmospheric Administration, 2011, National Climatic Data Center, temperature and precipitation, accessed September 13, 2012, at http://www ncdc. noaa.gov/temp–and–precip/time–series.

National Weather Service, 2011, National Operational Hydrologic Remote Sensing Center National snow analyses, accessed September 13, 2012, at http://www nohrsc noaa. gov/nsa/.

New Hampshire Department of Environmental Services, 2011, New Hampshire snow sampling sites, snow sampling data, accessed September 13, 2012, at http://www2.des.state. nh.us/RTi_Home/snow_sampling_stations.asp.

Olson, S.A., 2008, Estimation of flood streamflows at selected recurrence intervals for streams in New Hampshire: U.S. Geological Survey Scientific Investigations Report 2008–5206, 57 p.

U.S. Army Corps of Engineers, 2011, NEA Reservoir Regulation Section, New England District, NAE Snow Survey Bulletins, accessed September 13, 2012, at http://rsgisias. crrel.usace.army.mil/nae/cwmsweb.cwmsindex.

U.S. Geological Survey, 2011a, WaterWatch Past Flow/ Runoff: U.S. Geological Survey Web interface, accessed August 24, 2012, at http://waterwatch.usgs.gov/index. php?id=romap3&sid=w__graph.

U.S. Geological Survey, 2011b, WaterWatch Past Flow/ Runoff: U.S. Geological Survey Web interface, accessed August 24, 2012, at http://waterwatch.usgs.gov/index. php?id=romap3&sid=w__map.

U.S. Geological Survey, 2012, Water-resources data for the United States, water year 2011: U.S. Geological Survey Water-Data Report WDR–US–2011, site 04295000, accessed January 25, 2012, at http://wdr.water.usgs.gov/ wy2011/pdfs/04295000.2011.pdf.

Figures 5–15

01052500 Diamond River near Wentworth Location, NH

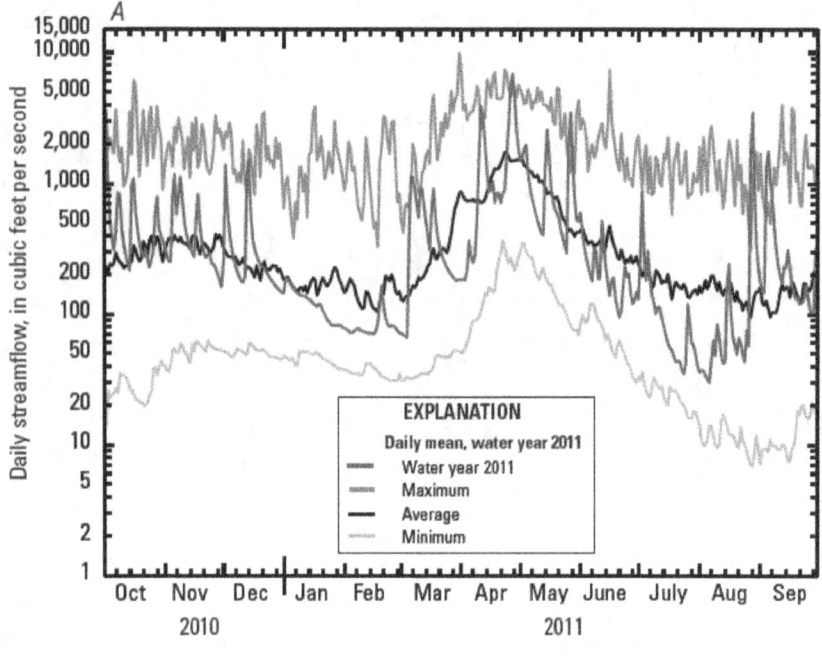

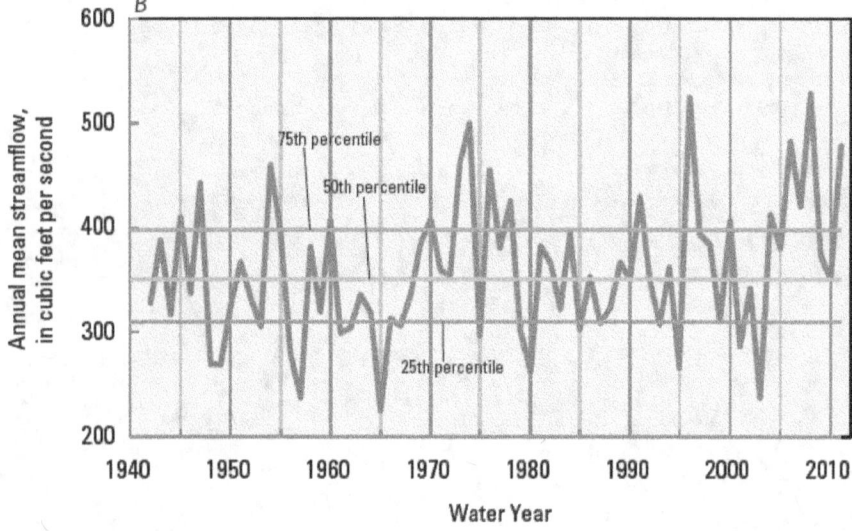

Figure 5.   *A,* Daily mean streamflow for water year 2011 and daily maximum, minimum, and average streamflows for water years 1941–2010 at station 01052500 Diamond River near Wentworth Location, New Hampshire, and *B,* annual mean streamflow for water years 1941–2011, and 25th, 50th, and 75th percentiles for annual mean streamflows.

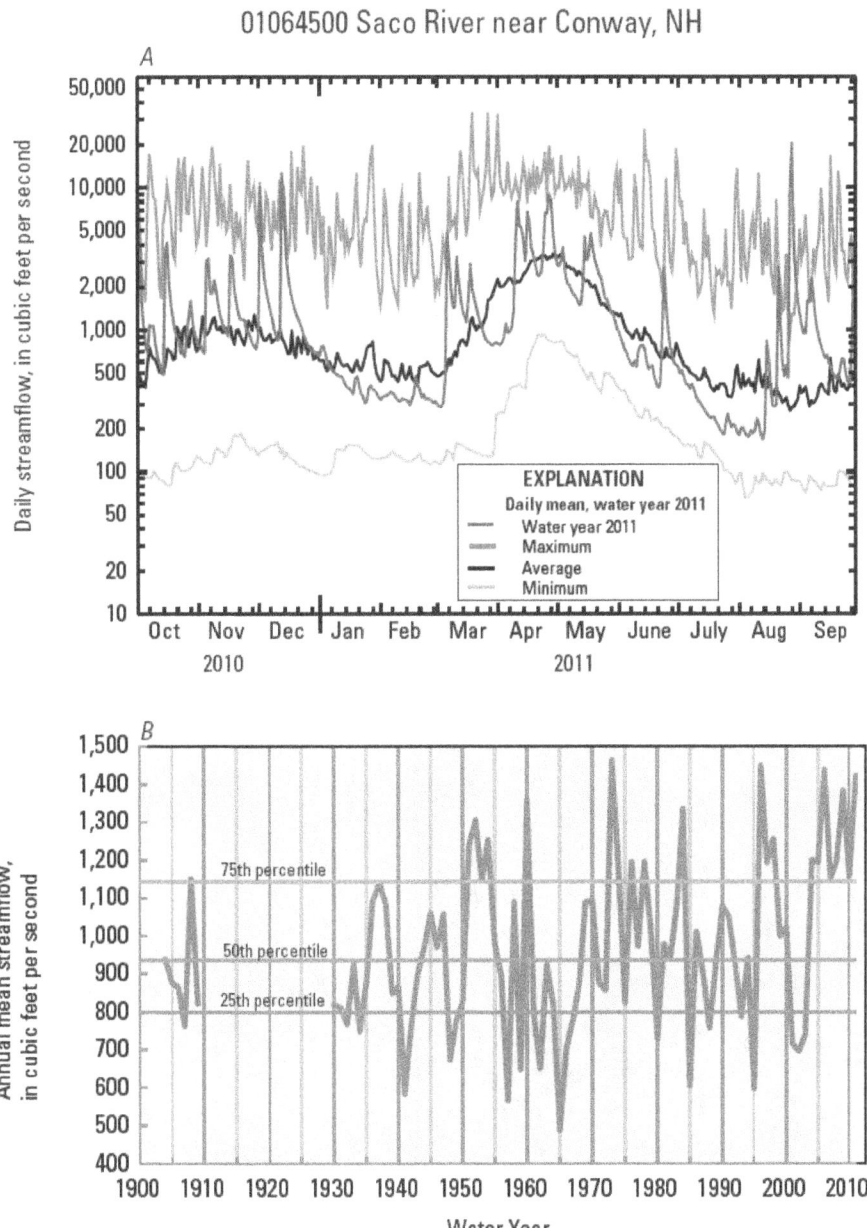

Figure 6. *A,* Daily mean streamflow for water year 2011 and daily maximum, minimum, and average streamflows for water years 1904–10, 1929–2010 at station 01064500 Saco River near Conway, New Hampshire, and *B,* annual mean streamflow for water years 1904–10, 1929–2011, and 25th, 50th, and 75th percentiles for annual mean streamflows.

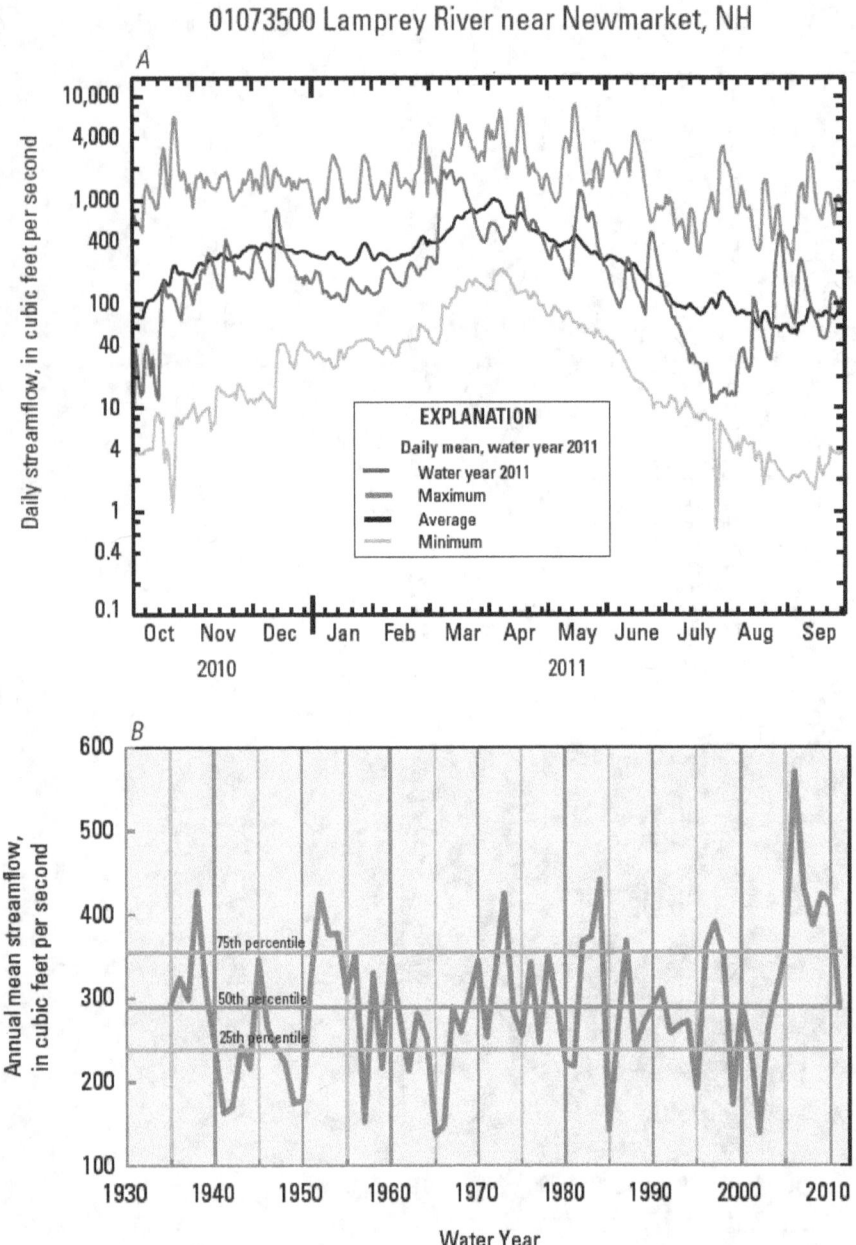

Figure 7. *A,* Daily mean streamflow for water year 2011 and daily maximum, minimum, and average streamflows for water years 1934–2010 at station 01073500 Lamprey River near Newmarket, New Hampshire, and *B,* annual mean streamflow for water years 1934–2011, and 25th, 50th, and 75th percentiles for annual mean streamflows.

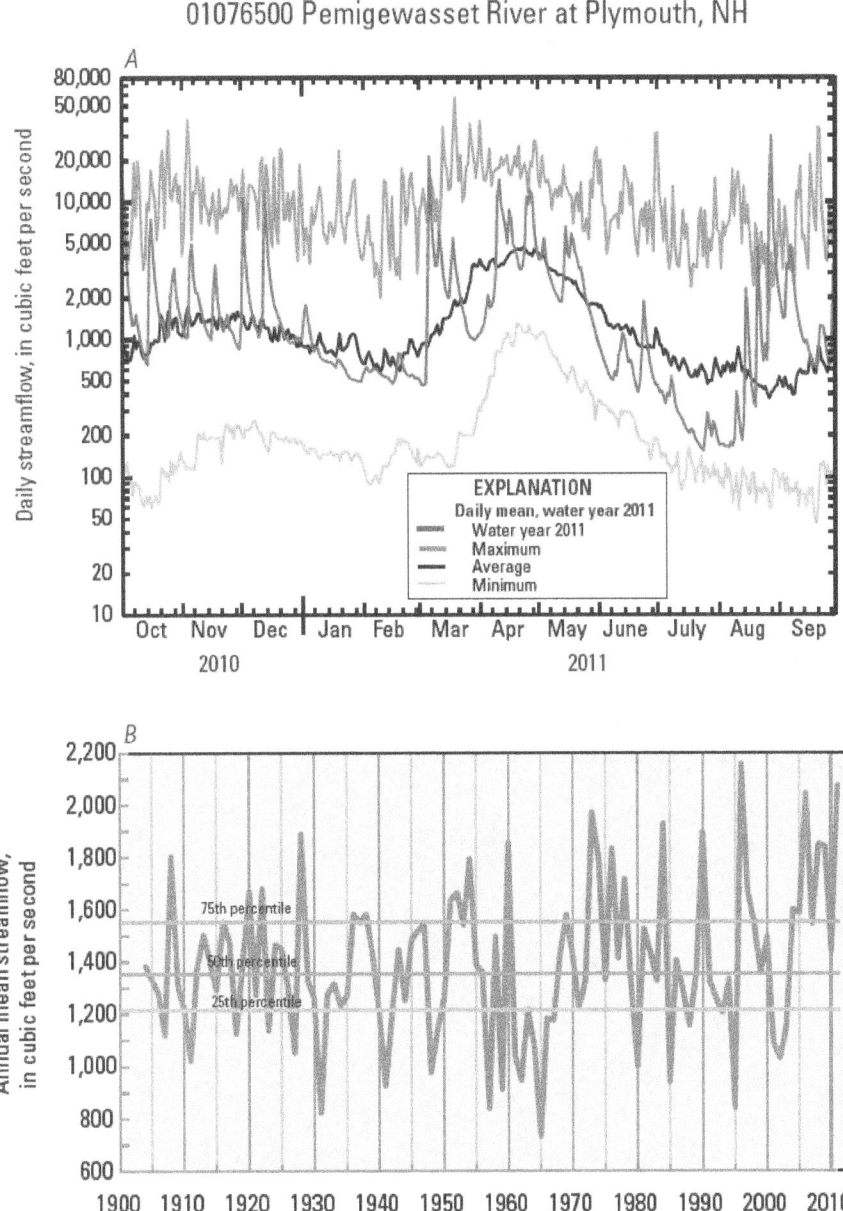

Figure 8. *A,* Daily mean streamflow for water year 2011 and daily maximum, minimum, and average streamflows for water years 1904–2010 at station 01076500 Pemigewasset River at Plymouth, New Hampshire, and *B,* annual mean streamflow for water years 1904–2011, and 25th, 50th, and 75th percentiles for annual mean streamflows.

01092000 Merrimack River near Goffs Falls, below Manchester, NH

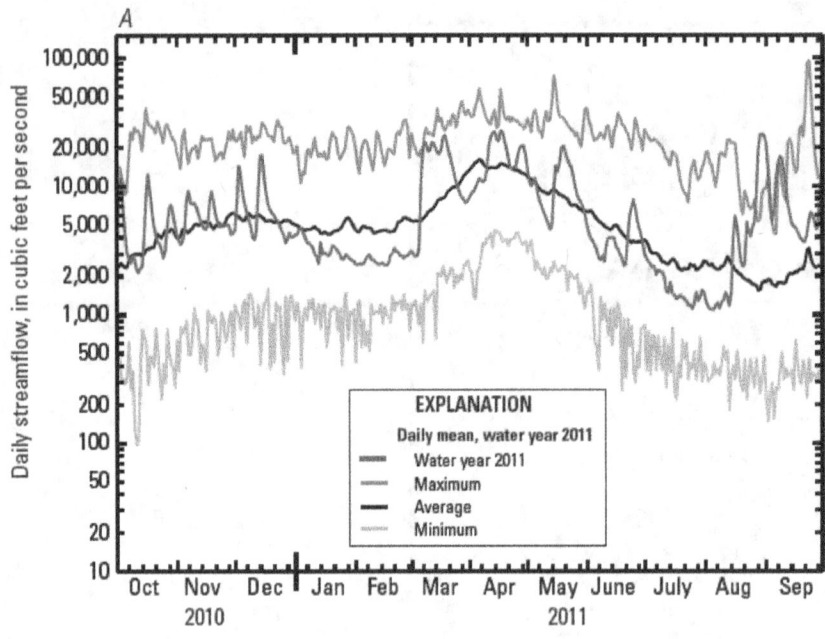

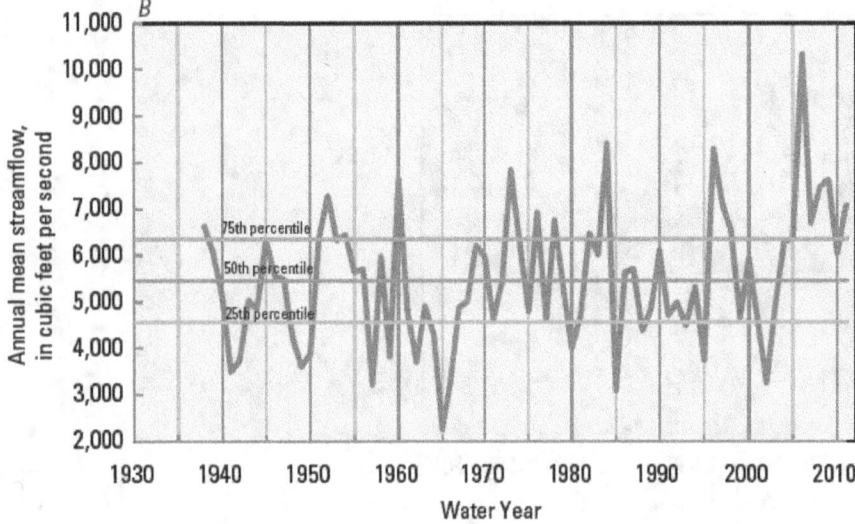

Figure 9. *A,* Daily mean streamflow for water year 2011 and daily maximum, minimum, and average streamflows for water years 1937–2010 at station 01092000 Merrimack River near Goffs Falls, below Manchester, New Hampshire, and *B,* annual mean streamflow for water years 1937–2011, and 25th, 50th, and 75th percentiles for annual mean streamflows.

01137500 Ammonoosuc River at Bethlehem Junction, NH

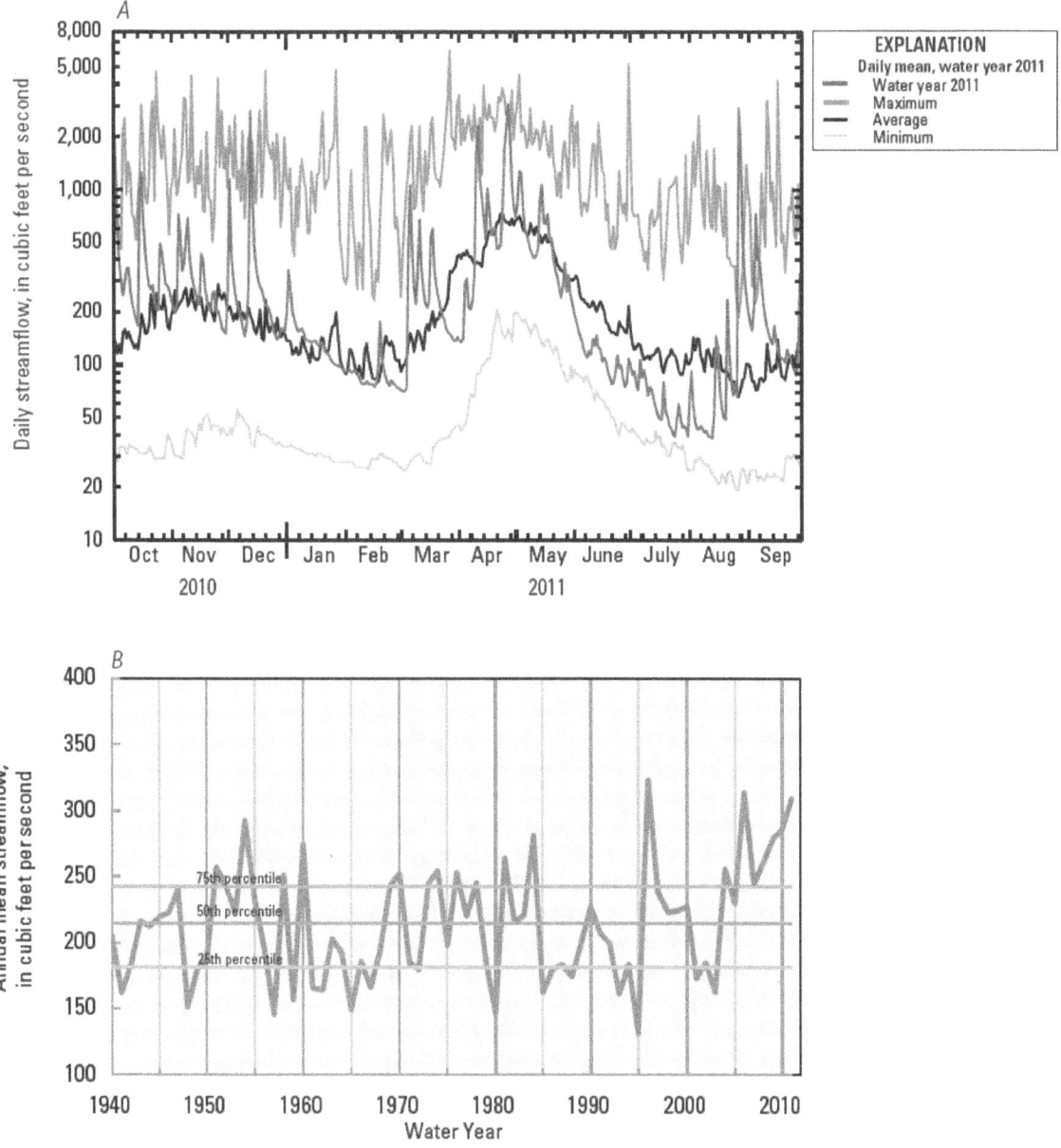

Figure 10. *A,* Daily mean streamflow for water year 2011 and daily maximum, minimum, and average streamflows for water years 1939–2010 at station 01137500 Ammonoosuc River at Bethlehem Junction, New Hampshire, and *B,* annual mean streamflow for water years 1939–2011, and 25th, 50th, and 75th percentiles for annual mean streamflows.

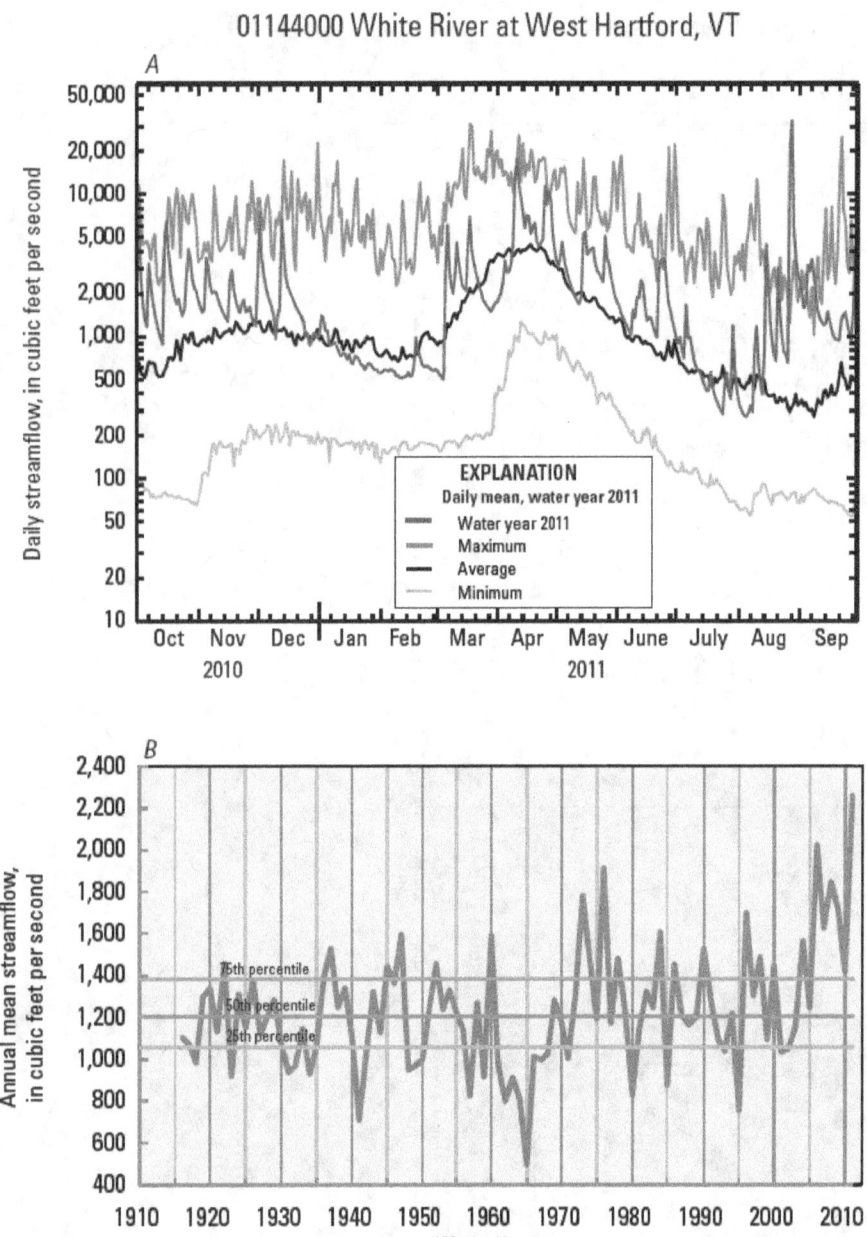

Figure 11. *A,* Daily mean streamflow for water year 2011 and daily maximum, minimum, and average streamflows for water years 1916–2010 at station 01144000 White River at West Hartford, Vermont, and *B,* annual mean streamflow for water years 1916–2011, and 25th, 50th, and 75th percentiles for annual mean streamflows.

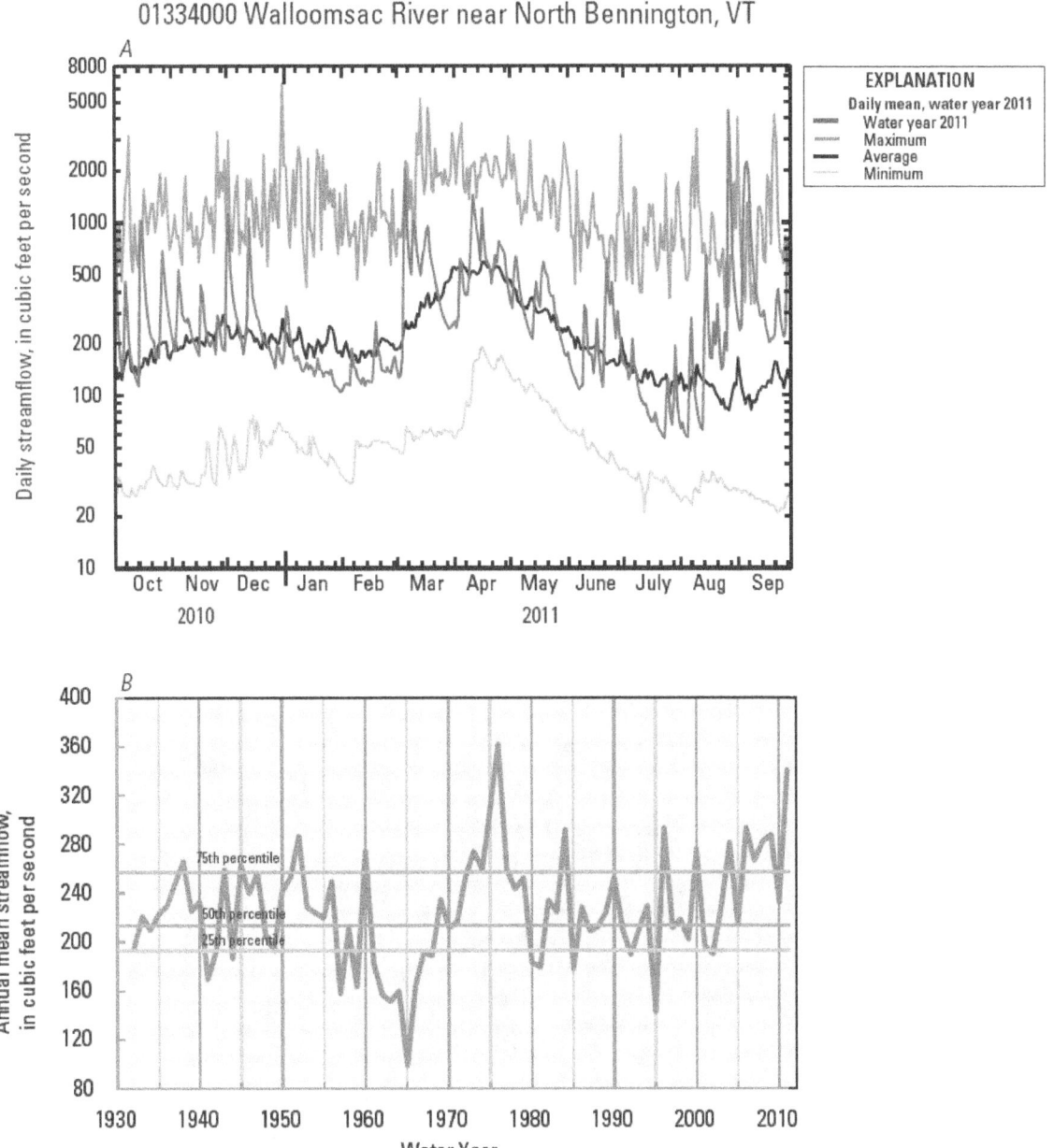

Figure 12. *A,* Daily mean streamflow for water year 2011 and daily maximum, minimum, and average streamflows for water years 1931–2010 at station 01334000 Walloomsac River near North Bennington, Vermont, and *B,* annual mean streamflow for water years 1931–2011, and 25th, 50th, and 75th percentiles for annual mean streamflows.

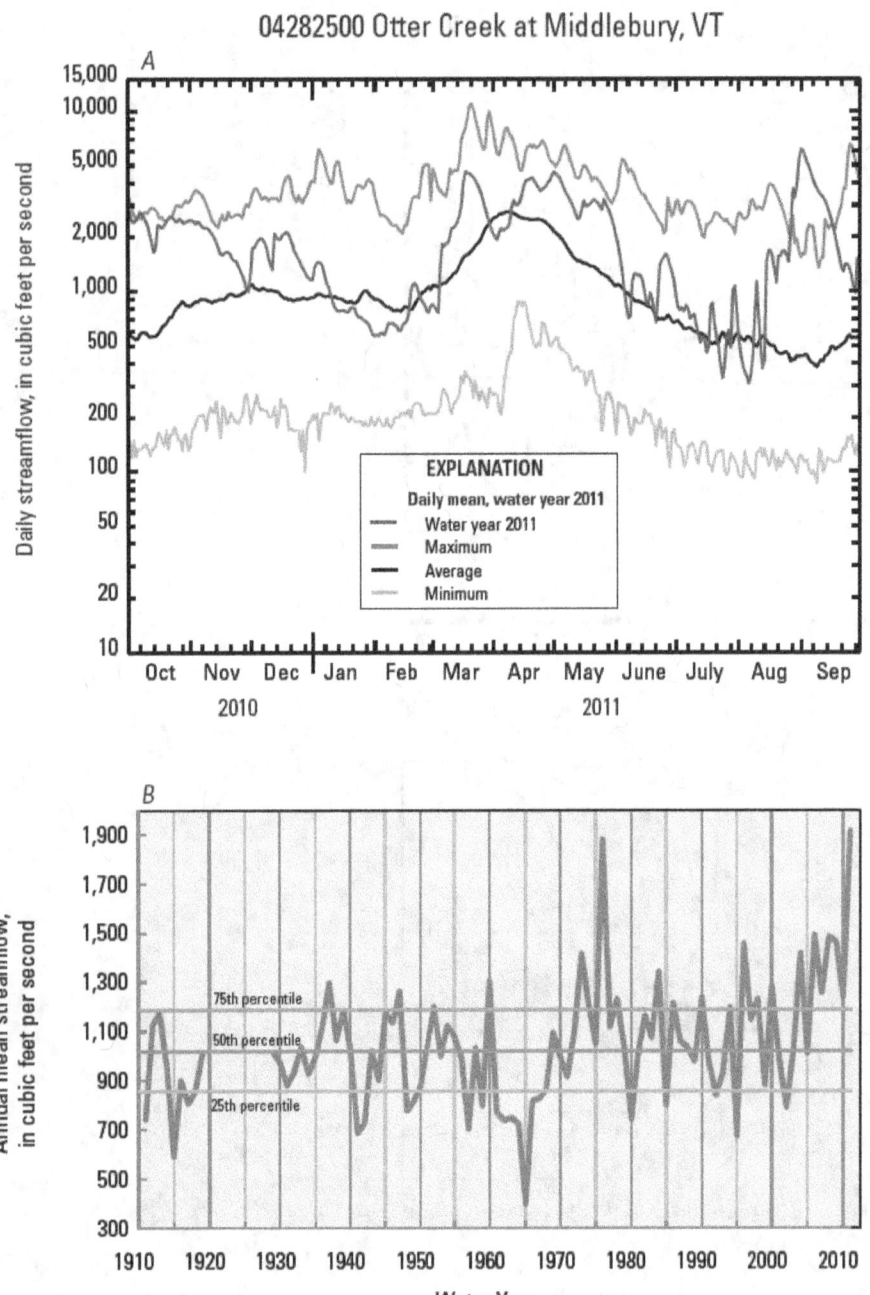

Figure 13. *A,* Daily mean streamflow for water year 2011 and daily maximum, minimum, and average streamflows for water years 1911–20 and 1929–2010 at station 04282500 Otter Creek at Middlebury, Vermont, and *B,* annual mean streamflow for water years 1911–20 and 1929–2011, and 25th, 50th, and 75th percentiles for annual mean streamflows.

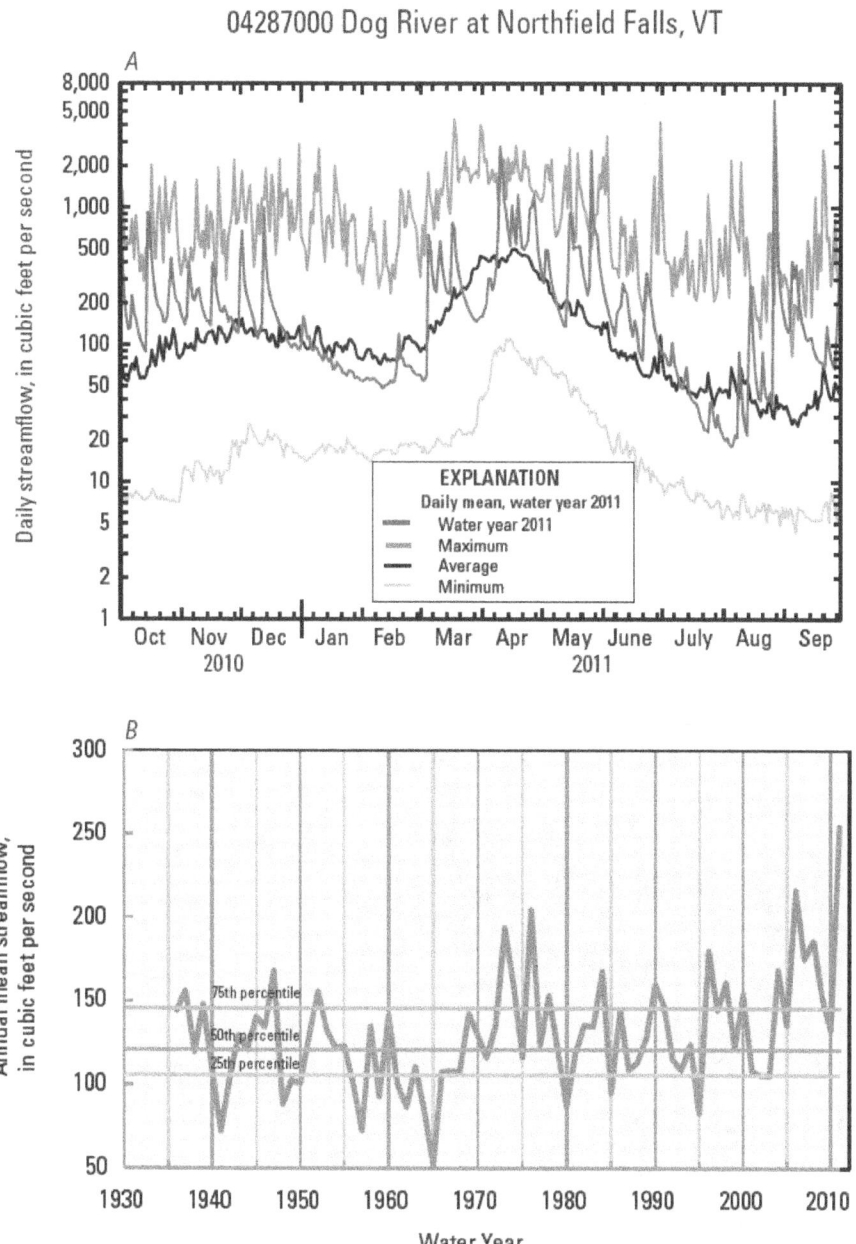

Figure 14. *A,* Daily mean streamflow for water year 2011 and daily maximum, minimum, and average streamflows for water years 1935–2010 at station 04287000 Dog River at Northfield Falls, Vermont, and *B,* annual mean streamflow for water years 1935–2011, and 25th, 50th, and 75th percentiles for annual mean streamflows.

04293500 Missisquoi River near East Berkshire, VT

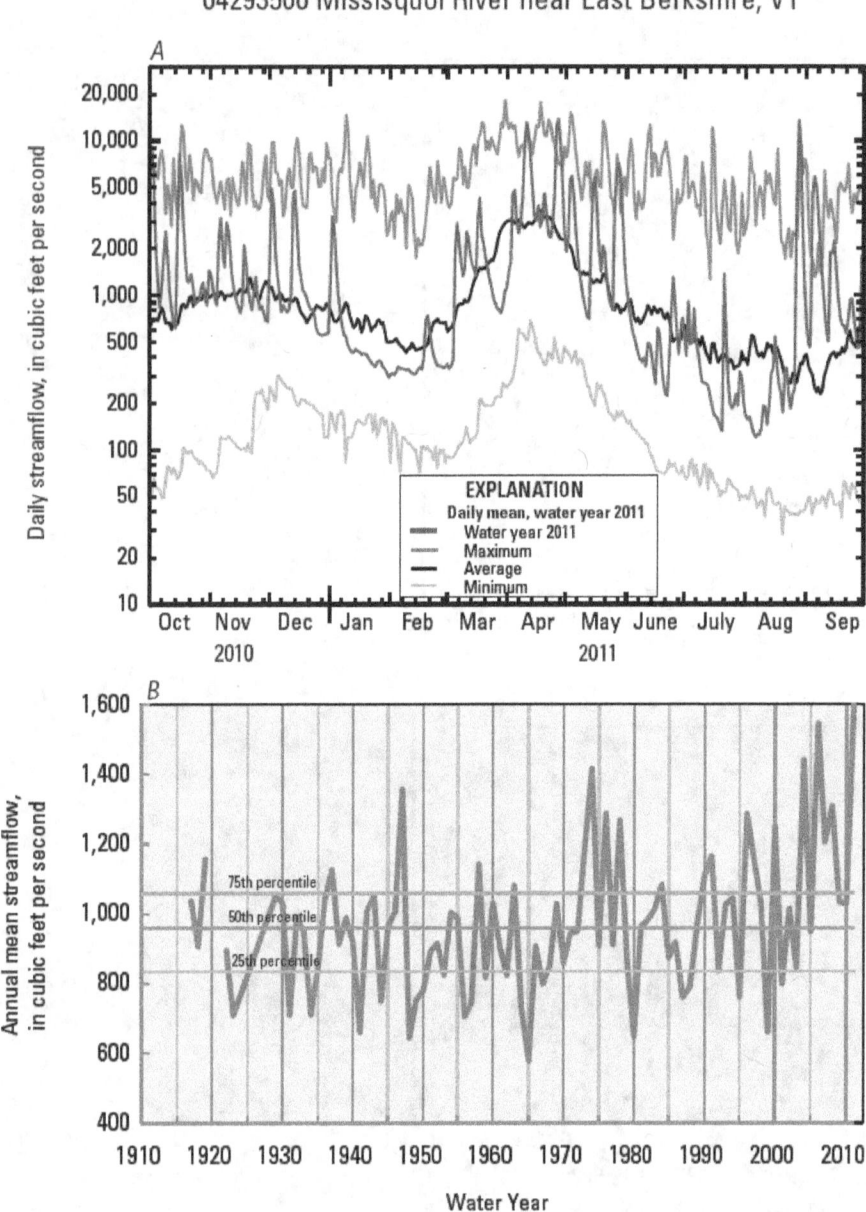

Figure 15.   A, Daily mean streamflow for water year 2011 and daily maximum, minimum, and average streamflows for water years 1917–19, 1922, 1923, and 1929–2010 at station 04293500 Missisquoi River near East Berkshire, Vermont, and B, annual mean streamflow for water years 1917–19, 1922, 1923, and 1929–2011, and 25th, 50th, and 75th percentiles for annual mean streamflows.

www.ingramcontent.com/pod-product-compliance
Lightning Source LLC
Chambersburg PA
CBHW080347290526
45791CB00009BA/2768